OWN
YOUR SPACE

The Woman's Guide to Polish, Poise and Empowerment

Nadia Bilchik and Lori Milner

Greater Impact Publishing

First published in 2016
by Pan Macmillan South Africa Private Bag X19
Northlands Johannesburg 2116
www.panmacmillan.co.za

ISBN 9 780 9885013 2 4
e-ISBN 978-1-77010-455-6

Editing by Kelly Norwood-Young
Cover and text design by Karen Lilje, Hybrid Creative
Author photographs by Emma O'Brien (Lori Milner) and Eric Bern (Nadia Bilchik)
American Team:
Editing by Michelle Watson, Topflight Communication
Text Layout by Bryan K. Reed, bryankreed.com

Contents

. . . .

INTRODUCTION

How do they do it?
You have surely noticed those women who walk into a room exuding unshakeable
self-assurance, those compelling women who seem to be able to achieve absolutely
everything. What is the magic that accelerates their careers, takes them to the next
level of management or enables them to take the plunge and start the business they
have always dreamed of?

Many ingredients go into the making of a successful career, but one of the most powerful is confidence. In the course of our own careers, as we've helped to empower thousands of women across the globe through our workshops, we have seen just how potent confidence is. We've unearthed these women's dreams and fears, and have given them the tools to boost their careers. Seeing first-hand the transformational effect of the most successful techniques, we've put together the ultimate toolkit in one book, so never again will a woman be without a mentor.

Whether you're a home executive or an entrepreneur, a student or a corporate jetsetter, whether you dream of getting into the corner suite or striking out on your own, the chapters that follow will give you the tools you need to envision the very best version of yourself ... and to *become* it. Some of the concepts we discuss may not always be revelatory, but there is often a gap between what we know and what we put into practice.

Therefore, *Own Your Space* provides a series of both new ideas and BLOs – *Blinding Lights of the Obvious* – the goal being to increase your awareness of the simple steps you need to take to accelerate your career:

- **Own your headspace** – Understand how your thinking, attitude and mindset have the greatest impact on your personal and professional life.
- **Own your physical space** – Master your physical presence, and learn how to leverage both your verbal and non-verbal communication skills to become more persuasive and engaging.
- **Own your interpersonal space** – Understand and elevate your EQ (emotional intelligence), develop strong relationships, and handle conflict with less stress and more confidence.
- **Own your virtual space** – Ensure that your online presence is enhancing the overall way you are perceived. This includes email etiquette as well as phone and social media usage.
- **Own your time** – Maximize your time and learn to prioritize in a way that is most productive.
- **Own your network** – Develop in-person and virtual networking skills to maximize personal and professional relationships.
- **Own your decisions, successes, failures, and finances** – Become a masterful decision-maker and understand the behaviors that have the potential either to enhance or to sabotage your career, and how both successes and failures can be beneficial. Learn to own your finances so they don't own you.
- **Own your ask** – Eliminate fear and uncertainty by learning the best way to ask for anything, from a raise to a promotion, in a comfortable and confident manner.
- **Own your podium** – Find your confident voice, overcome nerves and present information in a compelling, charismatic and persuasive way.
- **Words from women who own it** – Inspiring quotes and insights from accomplished individuals. Every quote is a gem of wisdom as our interviewees were as fearless about sharing their failures and vulnerabilities as they were about sharing their successes and what helped them to get there.

How to use this book

The best way to work with this book is to get a start-to-finish overview of all the tools, skills and insights across the entire spectrum of topics, and then to keep the book on hand when you need to make a major decision, rise above a mistake, bust some stress, or get more out of your day. Alternatively, when you are looking to negotiate a tricky deal, make a memorable first impression, network to build value-based relationships, or ask for a raise, we've got some pointers on those as well. You can refer back to the relevant chapter or simply review the summary action points at the end of each chapter.

More than anything, take what resonates and applies to you, and leave anything that doesn't. Before we are women, we are human; we can't be pigeonholed. While some of us have been socialized to be sweet and gentle and to conform to a stereotype, some of us have been actively encouraged to be fearless leaders. While some of us fall into that big statistical pool of women who won't try anything until we're over-prepared, some of us brazenly apply for that big promotion even when we know we're going to have to learn aspects of the job on the fly. Success is about knowing what the picture looks like to you personally, and then stepping into the fullness of that picture and discovering your true power. We look forward to taking you on a journey in which you will learn to truly *own your space* and grow into who you want to become.

1 Own
YOUR HEADSPACE

You want to feel that you have the power to bring your full, spirited self to the situation, stripped of the fears and inhibitions that might typically hold you back.

— AMY CUDDY

Forget what the glossy advertisements are saying. Your number one essential is not whatever the media decides is this season's must-have. Your number one essential is something deep within you. Your number one essential is your confidence.

Exuding a level of ease and confidence is more critical to your career success than you may think, because confidence has the power to create a self-fulfilling prophecy over and over again. Success may not be an easy journey for any of us, but when you're navigating your way to the next level, nothing in your toolkit is quite as potent as your self-confidence.

Confidence makes anything possible — professionally, intellectually, athletically, or socially. In *The Confidence Code* Katty Kay and Claire Shipman describe it as being life's enabler. They say that "success correlates just as closely with confidence as it does with competence, and that ultimately it is the characteristic that distinguishes those who imagine from those who do."

Confidence incites us to action. From voicing our opinion around the boardroom table to applying for a higher position or salary increase, confidence is the force that catapults us.

Even if you're not selling a product or a service, you're selling yourself. In every interaction with others, from the first moment you speak, write or act, you're constantly selling your personal brand. And that makes us all salespeople. You cannot expect anyone to believe in you if you don't believe in yourself. You cannot make someone else believe that you're amazing until *you* believe, deeply, unequivocally, that you are.

"I've never not done something because I was afraid," says global culture strategist Pollie Massey. "For me, it has been trusting the small inner voice, or that voice of my dad, telling me you're enough, you're more than enough, you were created to do great things. And I'm still fearful, sometimes, but I call them butterflies, and I say it's okay to have butterflies as long as they're moving in the same formation."

This kind of confidence is compelling, and it requires both mental and physical awareness. But it eludes far too many of us. In our extensive training, keynotes and workshops, we've found two things that most relentlessly cast shadows over women's self-confidence. One is our innate pursuit of perfection. The other is fear.

Fear is an invisible cage. It can imprison us in a perpetual state of inaction. It can prevent us from moving forward, moving up, or moving on. And it's not just one fear. Our fears can be many: the fear of failure, the fear of success, the fear that we don't belong, or of looking like a fool. We are often afraid of how others will perceive us, and of our own ambitions. Ultimately, we are terrified that we are just not good enough, a fear that often feeds a crippling drive for perfection.

As women, we often set the bar impossibly high, and feelings of inadequacy can gnaw at us constantly because, no matter what we do, we still think we'll never be good enough. While men are statistically more likely to take risks and leaps of faith even when they're unsure, unprepared or unequipped, women can fixate, obsess, overthink and sometimes even over prepare. We tend to hold back from applying for a position until we're more than qualified. We wait to submit a report until we've polished it so much we can practically recite it. Some of us hesitate when it comes to speaking up or presenting an idea until we know every fact. And even then, some of us still hold back.

Almost on a daily basis, we work with women who yearn for that naturally confident state that will free them from holding themselves back. The good news is that we *can* all be more confident. And we're not talking about fleeting, superficial confidence that stems from those moments you receive acknowledgment or approval from others. We're talking about the deep, internal, very real confidence that naturally develops when you truly start owning your space.

When you deeply own your relationship with yourself, your ambition, and your purpose, you begin to flourish. You become completely, authentically, unapologetically you. It's a journey to the best version of yourself and, like most journeys, it begins in the mind. Your mind shapes your reality, and any changes you want to make in your life need to be activated first within your internal world. You need to own your headspace.

So, how do we go about evicting the negative from our inner lives? Jack Canfield, best-selling author of *Chicken Soup for the Soul* and other similar titles, suggests that the first step is to take control of the thoughts you think, the images you visualize, and the actions you take. "How you use these three things determines everything you experience," he writes in another book, *The Success Principles*. "If you don't like what you are currently producing and experiencing, you have to change your responses. Change your negative thoughts to positive ones. Change what you daydream about. Change your habits. Change what you read. Change how you talk to yourself and others."

UNDERSTAND YOUR PAST CONDITIONING

When we want to own our headspace, we're naturally dealing with our thinking. But before we start to unravel our negative thoughts and limiting self-beliefs, we need to tear down the deep-seated conditioning that perpetually feeds the damaging perceptions we sometimes have of ourselves.

In our conversations with successful female leaders, they all had one thing in common, and that was their irrevocable belief that they had the right to be heard. They believed they were good enough and they deserved to be there. Sadly, far too many women believe just the opposite, and it goes much deeper than just a little dose of self-doubt. Many of us are unconsciously burdened with stifling self-beliefs that have been instilled and continually re-affirmed from girlhood.

From an early age, girls and boys are often encouraged to embrace different ideals. While boys play war and are taught to win, girls play house and are taught to co-operate. Society tends to reward little girls who are nice, sweet, polite, modest, selfless, and passive. Strong boys are lauded as born leaders, but strong girls are simply branded "bossy." It's a damaging psychological message that inhibits empowerment and stunts potential, both personally and professionally.

In fact, there's a marked disparity between the number of academically gifted and talented girls and the number of successful women. There is a disconnect somewhere between girlhood and womanhood. Rachel Simmons writes about it in her book *The Curse of the Good Girl*. She points out that girls talk, read and count earlier than boys, and that they're ready for schooling at an earlier age. In the early years, girls' IQ scores are higher, their grades are higher, and they have an edge over boys in academics at every level until the age of 14. And then everything shifts, and the balance reverses. In early childhood, gifted boys and girls are equal in number, but by adolescence, gifted boys outnumber gifted girls. Girls' self-confidence declines while feelings of hopelessness, discouragement and the drive for perfection grow. By adulthood, the number of men recognized as gifted far overshadows the number of women.

The gifted girls don't vanish into thin air. They're still there, but their talents become hidden or are sometimes consciously abandoned. Research conducted by Anita Gurian, PhD at the NYU Child Study Center, revealed that while gifted boys are among the most popular in school, gifted girls are often among the least. Girls are taught that it's important to be liked and in many cultures to be subservient, so instead of investing in their talents and being assertive, they start investing their time and energy into looking and behaving more and more like the "ideal" women they see on screen and in magazines. That's what society tells them to do.

Women who have grown up in very supportive environments often refer to parents, mentors or relatives whose encouragement was a source of inspiration. For example Naomi Nqweni, who heads the wealth management sector of a major Southern African bank, comes from a family who continually affirmed their children as they were growing up – girls and boys alike. Nqweni particularly remembers her uncle, whose gentle encouragement was always a source of inspiration for her. "Take it on, you can do it," he would say. To this day, Nqweni recalls her uncle's words whenever she encounters a challenge. She's made them her personal mantra, and she calls them to mind whenever she's facing something bigger than herself. And, because she realizes the value of being surrounded by people who enrich her power and potential rather than detract from them or undermine them, she has consciously created a circle of mentors and friends in her adult life – a circle she can tap into whenever she needs to. She affectionately refers to the circle as her Tribal Council.

Public relations executive Jenni Newman says she was also incredibly fortunate to have been raised by parents who believed in her. "Having the right attitude is absolutely vital," she says. "You can't walk into an interview and say, 'I'm not sure if I have the right qualifications.' On the other hand, I've hired people who have walked in and said, 'I know nothing about your business, but I am absolutely wonderful, and you are going to love me.'"

Whether your past conditioning was positive and affirming like Nqweni's and Newman's, or it was limiting in some way, or a little bit of both, the key is to understand what serves you and to discard anything that holds you back.

So, how do you overcome that past conditioning that is holding you back? One way is to work on what you are thinking. As yoga and meditation guru Paramahansa Yogananda says, "Since you alone are responsible for your thoughts, only you can change them."

When you understand how neural pathways are created in the brain, you get a better understanding of how to let go of habits and thought patterns that no longer serve you.

Have you ever noticed that when you drive to work you always go the same route, even if there are different ways you could go? This is because you have created a neural pathway in your brain that has produced this routine. Sometimes we even drive to this destination on "autopilot."

So how do you create a different pattern and habit? If you are driving somewhere routinely and consciously, think about going a different way. Make this change a few times, then this becomes your new habit and the new neural pathway is formed. The same process applies to our thinking patterns. In fact, when you consciously stop cultivating negative thought patterns by putting your focus on more uplifting and empowering thoughts or beliefs, the neural pathways associated with those old, negative thought patterns start to lose their hold over you, and you actively begin to forge new neural pathways in your brain – and that's when you start laying a solid foundation for some very real change.

EXERCISE: CHANGE YOUR CONDITIONING

Take some quiet time to reflect on your childhood. Look at what you've been told and been shown by your parents, teachers, community, siblings, and peers. This isn't a blame game – we're simply asking you to recognize your internal triggers in order to fully understand your relationship between your adult self and your inner child.

On an 8.5"x11" piece of paper (giving yourself space to write), use this table and the exercise below to reflect on your conditioning:

	Positive	Negative
Behaviors		
Beliefs		
Events		

- **Behaviors:** What did you do as a child that elicited accolades and rewards? What behaviors were you chastised for? For example, were you encouraged to contribute to dinner time conversation and to engage in interesting debate (which now enables you to speak out at the boardroom table), or were you expected to be quiet, subservient and to sit pretty (which now makes you feel that you have no right to voice your thoughts in a business meeting)?

- **Beliefs:** What ideas were you constantly told by those around you that empowered you? What was said to you that detracted from your power and potential? For example, were you told that you could do anything you set your mind to (which has become an internal belief that drives you to do the 'impossible' today), or were you told that to be valuable you had to be slim and pretty (which diminishes your confidence whenever you're surrounded by colleagues you perceive to be more attractive than you)?

- **Events:** What experiences limited you and what experiences made you feel indomitable? For example, did you receive a standing ovation at a school concert that now fuels your confidence as a compelling public speaker, or did you miss out on an opportunity because you were "too small" and today you just can't shake the feeling that you're insignificant and not to be taken seriously?

Once you've filled in the table, complete these steps:

- Pick the three conditionings that empower you the most from your positive column.
- Pick the three that most sabotage you and your career today from your negative column.
- Now turn them all into personal, present and positive affirmations: "You can't do anything right" could become "I can do anything I set my mind to." "Stop being such a control freak" could become "I am a born leader." "'To be worthy of anything, you have to be slim and pretty" becomes "I am enough." And "You're small and insignificant" becomes "I am a worthy being with boundless talent."
- Play around with your wording until you express your affirmations in a way that stirs a sense of optimism within you that makes you feel good, whole and strong.
- Write these affirmations down, and keep them somewhere you'll see often. Stick them on your office wall, make them the desktop background on your computer or plug them into your daily diary.
- Read them every chance you get.

This is how you start to rewire your brain. When thoughts are relentlessly played over and over in our minds and validated frequently by external events and internal emotions, they become unconscious patterns that shape the deep, internal sense of who we are, a core belief that we rarely stop to question. Because you're now on a path your mind perceives as the unknown, you need to carve out new, more productive patterns of thinking, steadily and repetitively. This is how recurring thoughts with a positive message have the potential to set up new patterns and pathways in your mind – pathways that can help you change your behaviors and enable you to make different choices.

OWN YOUR THOUGHTS

Your thoughts govern you. They're your internal programming and they color your perceptions, define your reality and control your behaviors and actions. Thoughts precede self-belief. Thoughts *become* self-belief. Every day, we meet and work with women who are burdened by negative thoughts. *I'm not good enough. I can't do this. It's impossible. I don't deserve this. Good things never happen to me. Other people are smarter, more attractive and accomplished.* These are the kinds of negative thoughts that can play like a tape recorder on a continuous loop, over and over and over again, quietly whispering words that can destroy self-confidence.

As the author Thomas E. Kida urges in *Don't Believe Everything You Think: The Six Basic Mistakes We Make in Thinking,* "These destructive words and thoughts feed your fear. That pounding heart, that fluttery feeling in your stomach, the headaches, the sweaty palms and even nausea – all these stem from fear." Fear is a powerful emotion, a primitive reaction designed to prevent us from doing things that might cause us harm – whether that threat is real or imagined. And while negative thoughts feed fear, the fear in turn gives the thoughts even more potency. It's a vicious cycle that can hold back even the most skilled, talented, capable women by sabotaging potential, opportunities and, ultimately, happiness.

It can be the fear of failure, or even the fear of success (because, what then?). There's the fear of what others will think (that's a big one for women, because as little girls we're often taught to be "nice," that it's important for others to like us). Or the fear that you can't be a good mother and have an amazing career at the same time, that you won't have enough time, that you're biting off more than you can chew, that maternity leave will ruin your career.

Even accomplished leaders feel fear from time to time. Grace Harding, Company Leader of a large restaurant chain, speaks openly about her own fears. Even as a young girl, Harding was always a leader. "But that doesn't mean that I don't face fear every day'" she says. "I have a huge responsibility in this position, and what drives me is my vision and my need to make a difference in people's lives. I know what I want to do, and I move forward with determination. Yes, I'm scared, but I'm also tenacious to a fault, and that keeps me walking through my fear. It is our own beliefs that hold us back."

"I would say that self-doubt is omnipresent, and it comes in different forms as you go through your career," says Michelle Livingstone, VP of Transportation at Home Depot who considers it vital to get out of her comfort zone. "My mantra is, if you're not living on the edge, you're taking up too much space."

Some of the most essential skills we can master are learning to manage our thoughts and work through our fears, because realistically, no matter how positive our thinking eventually becomes, or how brave and successful we are, there will frequently be elements of fear and self-doubt that lurk in the background.

We read many articles aimed at women like us that urge us to stop being so critical of ourselves. But this negative self-talk is often unconscious and we're not even aware it's happening. And it's not just in the way we bully ourselves; it's also the unconscious words and phrases that pepper our daily thoughts like: *I'd better; I must; I should have.* These phrases are commonly referred to as "Mind Sneakers" that create anxiety and cause us to put unnecessary pressure on ourselves. We can start the process of changing our negative thoughts by being aware of the words we use and consciously changing these phrases to *I want to; I can; I allow myself;* and *I deserve.* You'll be surprised at how these words can positively impact your thinking.

Whenever you reinforce positive self-talk with positive action, you're strengthening the impact on your neural pathways and truly paving the way for transformation. Canfield reiterates the importance of this kind of thinking. "Because our brain expects something will happen a certain way, we often achieve exactly what we anticipate," he writes. "When you begin to believe that what you want is possible, your brain will actually take over the job of accomplishing that possibility for you."

EXERCISE: CHANGE YOUR THINKING

Start becoming aware of what you're saying to yourself on a day-to-day basis, and keep a thought diary for the next seven days. Throughout this time, be conscious of your inner dialogue, and write down both the positive and negative things you're saying to yourself.

Highlight the thoughts that occur most often, and make note of the thoughts that stir the strongest emotions within you (again, both the positive and the negative emotions). In the process, work on becoming aware of the people, events and scenarios that make you feel "less than," those that trigger your critical thoughts.

- When your week of "thought watching" is up, make a list of your top three: the three negative thoughts that come up most and evoke the strongest emotions; the three positive thoughts that most empower you; and the three scenarios or people that you feel most daunted by. We're going to work with these first, as dealing with the biggest monsters will help you with the less significant ones.

- Now thought-replace, and do it to the power of three. Create three new, uplifting "power virtues." These are your best and most admirable qualities.
  - The first power virtue comes from the list you've already made of your most empowering thoughts. Pick one of your top three from that list.
  - Your second is a virtue that you know is true, but don't consciously acknowledge very often.
  - Your third is a virtue that, while true, is something you almost never allow yourself to admit.
  - Remember to keep your power virtue statements personal, positive and present. Your statements will begin with, "I am ..."
  - Now add these to your collection of positive affirmations – and keep them in a place where you can refer to them often. Whenever you start engaging in negative self-talk, remind yourself about your power virtues, the inherent qualities that you can rely on and draw strength from to get you through any road blocks along the way.
- When you're about to face one of your top three triggers (people or scenarios that make you feel "less than"), take a few minutes to prepare yourself. Consciously adapt your internal dialogue and gently remind yourself, despite your fears and your doubts, exactly why you are valuable and remarkably capable of doing what needs to be done right now.

The point of this exercise is to change the focus from negative, limiting thinking to thought patterns that nurture self-confidence, power and potential. If you find yourself starting to engage in an internal argument, warring between thoughts that are polar opposites, let it go, back away and take a break.

If you are still consumed by negative thoughts about yourself, psychologist Mario van Tonde suggests you follow this process:

- Stop, and challenge this negative thought. Ask yourself for the objective proof. For example, if you feel you don't deserve a promotion, ask yourself, *Where is the proof for this thought?* Most likely, there is none!
- The next step is to write out an apology to yourself. This may feel a bit strange at first, but it is imperative, as it allows you to take control of the negative thought. Forgiving yourself for self-critical thoughts, such as *I am not good enough*, allows you to liberate yourself. The act of acknowledging, apologizing and forgiving yourself helps to set up a protective boundary.
- The last step is to switch to a sense of gratitude. Shift your focus to the things you are grateful for in your life and use this as the basis to move forward.

- You can also pick up the phone and have a quick chat with a sympathetic friend, take a five-minute walk around the block, or take a page out of Nqweni's book and create your own Tribal Council – a supportive circle of mentors and friends you can tap in to whenever you need a little encouragement.

OVERCOME SELF-DOUBT

On the journey to success, it's inevitable that you will experience moments of self-doubt along the way. Your ability to own your space determines how you choose to deal with it. You can either let it paralyze you, or keep going no matter what obstacles come your way.

Nadia, who has been a broadcaster and professional speaker and trainer for the past 20 years, vividly recalls moments of terrifying self-doubt, "moments when I have broken out into a cold, heart-palpitating sweat in which my usual sense of breezy self-confidence just seemed to drain away. In fact, I had exactly that kind of moment just before I was scheduled to introduce media mogul, philanthropist and restaurateur Ted Turner, who was being honored by the Georgia Restaurant Association. *Am I the right person for the job?* I wondered. *How could I possibly do this justice?*

"Ten minutes later, I walked to the podium to warmly welcome Ted Turner to one of Atlanta's premier events – and received numerous compliments after the event for the "polish" and "warmth" of my performance. It was as if that paralyzing moment of self-doubt had never existed."

So, how do you deal with moments of self-doubt, times when you have a crisis of confidence and question your knowledge and ability? How do you transition to both feeling and projecting a sense of confidence and strength?

The first step is to remind yourself that you are not alone. Self-doubt is normal; these kinds of moments can and do happen to all kinds of people in many different situations. People on every level, from accomplished executives to seasoned classroom teachers, experience self-doubt, whether the task at hand is to address a room full of businesspeople or a class of boisterous teenagers.

The next step is to use the tried-and-true strategies of internal dialogue and visualization to re-establish your sense of your own power and strength. Honore de Balzac, a French novelist and playwright, wrote, "Nothing is a greater impediment to being on good terms with others than being ill at ease with yourself." Our inner dialogue – what we communicate to ourselves – has a huge impact on the way we project ourselves to the rest of the world. During times of self-doubt, you need to change the story you're telling yourself and skip to the next chapter.

When you feel anxious or you become aware of self-critical thoughts, it helps to take a deep breath and neutralize the adrenalin that is pumping through your system. Think back to positive moments from your life – what we call your Positive Emotional Memory Database™ (PEMD). Call to mind times when you've enjoyed accomplishments and experienced a sense of satisfaction. Start reflecting on memorable moments of triumph. These memories can be anything from the exhilaration of winning that tough competition, to securing a scholarship to your dream school or interviewing successfully to land that perfect job.

Nadia's most potent moment was when she had the opportunity to host the opening of the Cape Town SOS Children's Village with President Nelson Mandela, and it's exactly that moment that she brought to mind when she walked on the stage to honor Ted Turner. By recalling these past positive experiences, moments when you have felt especially empowered, you will be able to replace feelings of doubt with moments of triumph.

Andrea Quaye, a high level marketing executive, recalls that she has experienced moments of self-doubt, but has practical tools she implements to overcome them. "Moments of self-doubt are challenging because you find yourself playing at twenty percent. You say less and you are apologetic about your views. The solution I have adopted is, acknowledge the emotion and ask yourself, 'If I knew I was playing at ninety percent, what would I do?' You need to take away the emotion; have the implicit self-belief and just focus on what needs to be done."

This method works for Quaye, but the real power comes from knowing what works for *you*. You need to find your method of combatting self-doubt in those vulnerable moments.

Another very effective technique to prepare for the task at hand is one we learned from an Olympic champion who "plays a video" of the perfect dive in her mind, from standing up on the diving board to performing this perfect dive, as she's done before in other competitions. You can apply this to yourself: Visualize yourself making an impressive speech or presentation, and allow yourself to imagine what it *feels* like to do that. You will find yourself looking forward to the challenge – or at the very least, not dreading it.

Then there's the strategy of "attitude adjustment." John Kehoe, renowned international author, has earned worldwide recognition for his pioneering work in the field of neuropsychology. In his book *Mind Power*, he says that while most people believe they are only as good as their last experience, that is simply not the case. We are a culmination of all of our successes. This means that no single challenge you face will make or break you, even if it feels that way at the time. Keeping this in mind can help you regain your confidence during moments of self-doubt.

Once you have adjusted your attitude and re-established a sense of self-assurance, you can begin to craft your communication. You will be amazed at how an internal sense of confidence is externally visible. Remember, whether it is one person or 1, 000 people, your audience cannot see your self-doubt; they can only see what is presented to them. "Self-confidence follows success," says telecommunications entrepreneur Joan Joffe. "Success comes from achieving the goals we set for ourselves. Goals, which are different for everyone, should be realistic and attainable. One should try to cultivate a positive and optimistic outlook combined with determination and humility."

Suzan Johnson Cook, President Barack Obama's former United States Ambassador-at-Large for International Religious Freedom, shares this sentiment, "Be yourself, and don't apologize," she says. "Celebrate yourself and find places that celebrate you and not just tolerate you. Self-doubt is often part of the success journey, whatever that might look like for you, so be ready to tackle it head on and do not give up."

So, what about our fears? Nelson Mandela famously said that he'd learned that courage was not the *absence* of fear, but the *triumph* over it. How do we triumph over our fears, particularly when we feel overwhelmingly insufficient, that someone else (or something else) is bigger than we are, or that we're just not good enough? We build up a PEMD – a series of images that reminds us of our strengths and capabilities.

EXERCISE: CONQUER YOUR FEARS – BUILD UP A POSITIVE EMOTIONAL MEMORY DATABASE (PEMD)

Give yourself a quiet half hour, and do yourself the honor of remembering all your past achievements. Look back at every triumph you have had, both personally and professionally. When last did you do that, if ever?

- As a start, think of three experiences you have had over the last ten years that have been validating for you, three moments when you achieved something, when you were complimented, or overcame some difficulty. Unearth some of your most delightful, most exhilarating, most powerful memories. You're creating an inventory of every time you ever felt a sense of achievement. Every time you felt amazing, accomplished, comfortable, confident, whole, complete, and authentically you.
- Take yourself back to those defining moments. Immerse yourself in them. And remember how you felt.
- Now go fully HD. See those moments with absolute clarity. Make your mental image clearer, crisper, sharper. Make the colors brighter, more vivid. Enhance the sound. Add applause if you want to, and most importantly, recall your feelings. Make those emotions of triumph, joy, exhilaration, completion and happiness as tangible as you possibly can.
- Finally, 'pin' those memories into your mind with a click of your fingers, a clap of your hands or a long deep breath. This is now your trigger to recall those memories at will and to replay them whenever you need them.

Recalling positive past experiences and visualizing them before speaking up in a meeting, going for an interview or giving a presentation, is a powerful antidote to nerves and fear. We tend to focus on our insecurities and to downplay our successes. So often, we start believing in our own mediocrity and forgetting just how accomplished, skilled and talented we really are. With your PEMD, you enable yourself to shift your focus to what you do well, and by doing so you remind yourself of your competence. As Kehoe says, "You allow success to literally vibrate within you."

GET COMFORTABLE WITH BEING YOU

So there you are. In a room full of people you admire, people you would like to show an interest in you, who could open doors of untold opportunities and become valuable partners in your life. But you find yourself coming across awkwardly and all wrong, or you take cover in the corner.

We might have fears of being judged; we may harbor doubts and uncertainties and have feelings of not measuring up. It's an uncomfortably acute sense of self-awareness, a feeling of lack and not belonging, and it radiates out from us in waves, eroding any chances we have of presenting ourselves as strong, capable women.

In many cases, it's our relentless pursuit of perfection that's at fault. While you may think that striving for perfection makes you a better person, more worthy, more prepared, and better equipped, the truth is it doesn't.

"As women, it's easy to lose track of what brings joy, and it's all tied together with being perfect," says Cynthia Good, founder and owner of Little PINK Book. "You can't be perfect for everybody else and own your heart."

Author and social research professor Brené Brown sums it up perfectly when she says that "acute perfectionism is a self-destructive, addictive and exhausting belief system." Healthy striving is self-focused: *How can I improve?* Perfectionism, on the other hand, is other-focused: *What will they think?*

She goes on to say that perfectionism actually hampers success. And she's got the research to prove it. In fact, perfectionism is often the path to depression, anxiety, addiction, and life paralysis. Brown urges women to stop hustling for other people's approval; to own our stories (even the messy ones); to lay down the "perfectionist" shield and ultimately to embrace our vulnerabilities and imperfections so that we can make the journey from *What will people think?* to *I am enough.*

Brown also says that the unremitting quest to be perfect is a distinctly feminine trait. We want to be perfect so badly that we obsess about everything, including our performances as mothers, wives, daughters, sisters, friends, bosses, and careerists. We wait until we're as close to perfect as we can get before attempting many or all of these.

And even then we often still don't think we're quite good enough.

We are our own worst judges. We end up standing in our own way. We set standards that we can never meet. We cripple ourselves because we set the bar impossibly high. What's worse is we have double standards for ourselves: what would be acceptable for a friend does not ring true with us. We are completely conditional when it comes to accepting ourselves.

Do yourself a favor and try to let go of all that perfectionism. Right now. Don't over-analyze yourself, don't aim for perfection, don't judge yourself, and stop worrying about what other people are thinking about you...because as, Don Miguel Ruiz writes, "They're all too busy starring in their own movies." It's true. Others don't actually view you through the same microscopic lens through which you scrutinize yourself.

To feel comfortable in your own skin is to feel safe and unthreatened. It means hushing the inner critic and releasing unrealistic goals of perfectionism. It means being gloriously authentic and believing you are enough, irrespective of your education, financial situation or background. Brown urges us to have the courage to be imperfect. Have the courage to accept yourself for the being you are right at this very moment.

Oscar Wilde, playwright and poet, famously said that you should just be yourself because "everyone else is already taken." So be you. And give yourself permission to be the *you* that no one else can be.

EXERCISE: GIVE YOURSELF PERMISSION

That's it. It's really that simple.

- Give yourself permission to be imperfect.
- Give yourself permission to be your authentic self.
- Give yourself permission to be right here, right now. Wherever you are.
- Say it. Right now. "I give myself permission to be here..."
- When you're faced with a daunting task, or meeting someone you perceive to be more worthy than you in some way, give yourself permission to be there with them, and to do the job you need to do, as you are, right at this very moment.
- Give yourself permission to be powerful.
- Give yourself full, boundless and complete permission to be happy, successful, fulfilled, content, beautiful, and spectacularly, authentically, imperfectly, perfectly you.

This is probably the most deceptively simple, most powerful and most liberating tool you can own as a woman. Take it, use it, and use it often.

OWN YOUR ATTITUDE

As we've said, in order to truly own your headspace, you need to own your thinking and be aware that your thinking dictates your attitude. In our interviews, the number one trait hiring managers said would make a candidate stand out was attitude. You can always teach skills, but you can never teach attitude. Your attitude is essentially the way you view the world, your place in it, and in turn, the way the world views you. You can have great skills and the best qualifications, but if your attitude is bad, no one will want to work with you.

In fact, many of the successful women we interviewed focused on the importance of attitude in their career trajectories. "I think the main quality that has helped my career acceleration is enthusiasm and a positive, can-do attitude," says Livingstone. "Early in my career, and still today, I'm willing to do any task, big or small, glamorous or not. And I think that willingness to jump in and roll up my sleeves has really helped."

Think about what attitude you decided to wear to work today. We all have a choice. We can choose an inner dialogue of self- encouragement and self-motivation, or we can choose one of self- defeat and self-pity. We all have this power. In times of hardship, the key is to realize that it's not what happens to you that matters, but how you choose to respond.

Mary Phakeng, who holds a senior research position at a large university, shares an inspiring analogy on how to take control of our attitudes to get through the difficult times that challenge us: "In life, you are always on stage and there are two concert halls. In one hall sit haters and in the other sit your likers or advocates. No matter what you do, these two audiences are always watching. The problem is that people in the concert hall of advocates are not very noisy, but quiet. They clap and they smile, but the sound of applause is soft. The concert hall that makes noise is the auditorium of haters; it is piercing. That is the reaction you hear all the time; the overbearing negativity that can make you lose confidence in yourself. When you hear it, it is very easy to forget there is a concert hall full of people who like you, an auditorium that probably even has more people in it.

"I often have to remind myself about this auditorium full of supporters. These people are cheering and want me to focus on my success. I don't want to disappoint them so I am going to keep going.

"Remembering that other people are rooting for me helps me when I support younger people. I say to myself, *I am in the auditorium of likers but it is too quiet so I am going to be louder.* I like being the one who says to the younger person doing her/his best, 'You are doing great, you go forit.'"

OWN YOUR HEADSPACE...IN A FLASH

- Rewire your brain by introducing new, positive self-beliefs and reinforcing them with actions as often as you can.
- Create a list of your power virtues and use them to replace your negative self-talk.
- When you experience a self-critical thought, take these four steps: Stop and challenge the negative thought, apologize to yourself, forgive yourself, and switch to a sense of gratitude.
- Accept that self-doubt is part of the journey to success.
- Build your PEMD and replay it every chance you get.
- Be fully aware that you determine your thoughts and your thoughts determine your attitude.
- Give yourself permission.
- Don't forget that somewhere out there is an auditorium full of "likers" who are rooting for you and cheering you on!

2 Own
YOUR PHYSICAL SPACE

Your body language, your eyes, your energy will come through to your audience before you even start speaking.

– PETER GUBER

We're often told not to judge a book by its cover. But that's what people frequently do. We make snap judgements all the time, and while we may not be making those assessments on a conscious level, they have a deep impact on our perceptions.

In fact, every day is an opportunity to reframe other people's perceptions of you. Every day is another opportunity to persuade, influence, motivate, attract, and inspire the people around you.

University of California, Los Angeles Professor Albert Mehrabian, a pioneer in the understanding of communications, found that over 90% of the way a message is received can be through non-verbal cues. This means that whether you're walking into a room or stepping up to a podium, standing in front of a crowd, waiting for a lift, sitting in a meeting or just hanging around the coffee machine, people are developing an impression of you before you utter a single word. The persona you project on a day-to-day basis could either significantly accelerate your career or sabotage it.

Look at those whose careers have soared. Their edge doesn't just come from their work performance. It's in the way they project themselves, in the positive perception they create, their confident body language, the conviction with which they speak, the way they connect with people, and how deeply they inspire us. Everything about them conveys authority and approachability, passion and energy.

Carolyn Jackson, former Chief Human Resources Officer at Coca-Cola, talks about using confidence and attitude to overcome negative stereotypes, too. "I've always demonstrated my confidence," says Jackson. "Do not be the stereotype they expect you to be – that would be loud, angry, whipping your head around. Just don't do it. Make sure you demonstrate facts, be articulate, and hold your ground."

That deep desire to make a real difference, to become the very best version of yourself – that's what lies at the core of your professional presence. And when you start to radiate that presence outwardly with poise, polish and authenticity, that's when people start to pay attention to you.

That's when you start to stand out.

The messages you're sending every day can be shaped by the way you choose to dress, the way you hold yourself and the way you connect with others. So you may as well send out a message that projects the best version of yourself.

It's a complete myth that if you weren't born with "it" you'll never have it. *Anyone* can work on creating a more professional presence. *Anyone* can work on building a stronger personal brand. It all starts with knowing who you are, what you want, and what your vision for yourself is. Then, you will be in a position to do everything you can to own your physical space and embody that vision.

Reframing other people's perceptions of you starts with the little things that some might consider superficial, like style, and verbal and non-verbal communication.

OWN YOUR STYLE

You are a free being, and you can wear whatever you want. Whatever makes you most comfortable. Whatever expresses your personality. But here's the truth: People judge us by our attire. The clothes we wear tell other people stories about ourselves, and if we want to utilize every tool at our disposal, we need to be aware of that.

So what are you wearing right now? What does it say about you as a professional? Does it say, *I've got it together; I know what I'm doing; I am capable, confident and competent?* Or, are you communicating different messages, like *I don't really care; I'm a mess; I don't really have it together; I don't think personal care is that important.*

OWN YOUR PHYSICAL SPACE

You could be highly capable, but that message can easily be lost in a sea of assumptions based on the way you dress and the way you choose to present yourself physically to the world.

There's a reason pilots wear uniforms. Pilots are really just everyday human beings flying other human beings in gigantic metal machines 30,000 feet above sea level at average speeds of 500 miles an hour. We place a lot of trust in our pilots, and their distinct, professional and groomed physical presence helps us do that. Would you feel as confident on the plane if your pilot was wearing stained tracksuit pants and a ripped, oversized jersey? You may not.

While you can and should retain your individuality, you need to be conscious of your company's dress policy and respect the environment you are in. If you are in the corporate world, or you have to dress in a uniform, so be it. It is the job *you* chose, and however you choose to express yourself, remember that ultimately you are representing the company, which means both acting and dressing professionally.

Even in the more relaxed and creative environments like advertising agencies, a sharper wardrobe can help distinguish you from the crowd and create a positive impression. Just because you don't see clients, doesn't mean that you don't have to put any thought into your wardrobe. It's not only the clients you need to impress; it's your bosses and your colleagues too. You don't want to get passed over for a promotion because the way you dress indicates a lack of caring or you don't "look" like you could be a leader. Good grooming is not just about making a polished first impression; it's about signaling to your boss, your team, colleagues, and yourself, that you're capable of bigger things.

Michelle Livingstone says she follows the "age-old recommendation" of dressing for the level you aspire to. According to Sylvia Ann Hewlett, author and leading expert gender and workplace issues, the rule of thumb is that you should look appropriate for your environment and, at the same time, be authentic to yourself. Clothes that feel inauthentic and aren't "you" actually detract from your internal sense of confidence as well as your professional presence. If you want to present an image of confidence and credibility, pay attention to your environment. Get inspiration from the female leaders and other role models around you. Experiment with looks that work for you, know yourself. As Focus Brands CEO, Kat Cole, puts it, become "less obsessed with looking 'incredible' and rather strive to look 'credible.'"

OWN YOUR WARDROBE

- **Dress for the job you want, not the job you have:** Dressing like a leader makes it much easier for others to picture you in that position. Show them you're ready.
- **Use a full-length mirror:** It's important that you're able to see how you look head to toe. Are you conveying the right message?
- **The blazer-and-heels effect:** In our experience, whether they are worn with jeans, pants, or a skirt, a tailored blazer and a pair of heels can instantly give you an aura of being pulled together and having authority. The blazer adds structure while the heels bring a little height and elegance.
- **The professional look:** Our advice is to strengthen your air of professionalism by avoiding dressing provocatively (with regard to your hemline, cleavage and undergarments).
- **Hair, makeup, nails, and skin:** Good grooming gives the impression that you're in control. Clean hair, manicured nails and a touch of makeup always look good, so consider investing in a good foundation (to even your complexion), and defining your features with a little slick of lipstick and mascara. If you don't like to wear makeup, it is still essential that your skin looks as good as possible so we would advise spending some time on a good skincare regimen.

Elaine Sterling, Director an Aesthetics Institute in Atlanta, says that if you concentrate on your skincare, you don't need makeup. A daily regimen can give you clear, glowing skin. Sterling also says moisturizer is a must, to give your skin a healthy glow and keep it hydrated. To get a fresh, clean look, choose a moisturizer with light-reflecting properties so your skin looks healthy and glowing, even without highlighter, foundation, blush, or bronzer.

Tara Young, the head of CNN makeup worldwide says, "Groom your brows." Without eye shadow, eyeliner and mascara to add definition, correctly shaped brows can provide definition and help frame your face, giving you a more polished look. That way, she says, you can have a very natural look and still be professional, stylish and groomed.

- **Fragrances and accessories:** A signature scent can be good, and accessories can be wonderful expressions of you, but keep it subtle. Don't let anything overpower you or detract from your presence.
- **Add a dash of individuality:** Even in a highly corporate environment, there are creative ways you can represent your personal brand. It is possible to retain your freedom of expression in your wardrobe while respecting the culture of the company you work for. Scarves, brooches, glasses, and shoes are a great way to bring a pop of color and personality.
- **Be authentically you:** Not a makeup and heels kind of person? Then ditch the makeup and heels! The only person in control of the perceptions your physical presence creates is you. Take what works for you and leave the rest.
- **Embrace your femininity:** It is our experience that the amount of credibility and authority you want to convey is directly proportional to the formality of your attire, but that doesn't mean you need to wear a 1980s-style power suit. You can wear something that is feminine but maintains a credible presence. Remember that your outer appearance needs to be a reflection of who you truly are.

GIVE YOUR WARDROBE THE SPF

- **Structure:** Whatever the dress code, remember that clothing with defined lines and structure will almost always look sharper and more professional. Structure conveys authority, reliability and control, so make sure your wardrobe includes shirts with collars and at least one structured jacket. Choose clothes with clean lines and keep options in classic colors like navy, grey and black.
- **Proportion:** Learn to balance your presence. Tall and large women already have a more significant presence, so bright colors and big buttons may actually have an overwhelming effect, whereas accessories and details in clothing can give petite women a bigger presence.
- **Fit:** Know your body and how clothes fit you. You don't want to be popping out of your outfit, but you don't want to look like you're wearing a curtain either. If you have doubts about what works best for you or you have any issues with your body image, ask for expert advice from a personal image consultant or hop online for some free tips.

Your wardrobe is one element of your personal brand that's relatively easy to fine-tune. As Hewlett says, "Your business attire is your armor." It should give you the confidence to stand taller, reflect your inner conviction and make you feel invincible.

"For better or worse, we make judgements about people just by looking at them," says Jenni Newman. "Some people have a natural presence and they walk into a room and own it, while others have to work at it. But there's nothing worse than apologizing for yourself all the time. The way you speak and work the room when you walk in is something that grows and improves the more you do it. Presence is a gift, but is also a skill and you need to work hard at it, but make it look effortless."

OWN WHAT YOU SAY – VERBAL COMMUNICATION

So, you've pulled together a suitable wardrobe that says, "I am capable, confident and competent." Fabulous. Now, you need to reinforce that image with the words you speak.

There is no question that leaders need to communicate clearly. And, of course, so do *potential* leaders. Whether it's in the office, around boardroom tables, at dinner parties, or at client functions, each and every interaction contributes to the overall way you are perceived.

At its core, communication is simply about sharing information and expressing ideas. Your ability to articulate and present yourself in a public arena with clarity, confidence and charisma is critical to your career success. We've seen many talented individuals sabotage themselves when they don't speak up in meetings or don't take the opportunity to showcase their strengths and make their points in a public forum.

We all may not be born with perfect public speaking skills, but there's nothing stopping us from becoming *better* speakers (we will share the *how* in Chapter 9). We can all learn to express ourselves more clearly, speak with conviction and, in so doing, build a more compelling personal brand.

One of the surest ways to become a better speaker is to be thoroughly prepared. Make sure you know everything you can within your area of expertise. Take the time to research the latest trends, find out what's happening elsewhere and what other companies are doing. This way, when you speak, not only will you have something interesting to say, you'll also be speaking from a solid knowledge base.

And when you're done researching everything you can about your field, research something else. People love well-rounded individuals, so work on developing a little knowledge on a wide variety of subjects. Start with topics that you're most passionate about, whether it's art, gadgets or long-distance running. Then broaden your scope and move on to easy-to-talk-about, general-interest topics like movies, books, food and current affairs.

And then read a little more, whether it's fiction, non-fiction, news articles, or poetry. Good writers pay close attention to words and the effects that those words have. Just by reading their works, you can learn from them, enhance your vocabulary and find more captivating ways to express your own ideas. Even if the thought of getting out there terrifies you, remember that the more clearly you can communicate, the more you expose yourself to potential opportunities. We know that the corporate world can be ruthless, but you still have to go out there and shine. So, even if you feel concerned or anxious about how people will respond, take that chance, say what you have to say, and *own* it!

OWN WHAT YOU SAY

- **Be your authentic self:** Speak from your heart. Be honest and be genuine. People respond to the real deal.
- **Manners matter:** Say please and thank you – even when somebody's just doing something they're paid to do. Remember people's names, use the titles they worked so hard for and never, ever interrupt when someone else is speaking.
- **Mind what you're shutting down:** Don't be the one who always says no. *But. Never. Impossible. It can't happen.* These are words that shut down people, ideas and proposals without offering a way forward. Be the one who is open to finding a solution – don't be out to prove a point.
- **Steer away from gossip:** Office gossip, celebrity gossip, political gossip – it's all essentially the same. And as the adage goes, "Strong minds discuss ideas, average minds discuss events, weak minds discuss people."
- **Words you can do without:** Don't cloud your language with fillers like "um," "uh," "you know," and slang, or expletives (those four-letter words you weren't allowed to use on the playground are just as inappropriate in business). They detract from your physical presence. Fillers can make you seem indecisive while slang and expletives can be interpreted as disrespectful, unprofessional and even aggressive.

- **Words you can grow:** Is everything always "fabulous" or "awesome"? Nobody's saying you need to become a walking thesaurus, but try to find different ways to express yourself every now and then. And don't be afraid to expand on *why* you like the idea and why you think it'll work. It's an opportunity to show others your deeper understanding of the bigger picture and all the factors at play.
- **Be a giver:** If someone deserves an accolade or a moment in the spotlight, give it to them. Be generous with those around you and give them the support they need.
- **It's not always about you:** You don't have to be the one talking all the time. Ask questions. Show genuine interest in the people you're in conversation with. Listen.

THE POWER OF HOW

- **Slow down:** No matter how busy or self-conscious you are, don't rush through whatever it is you're saying. Pace yourself. What you have to say is of value, and so is the person you are speaking to. So take your time. You'll come across calmer and more put together. Plus, it gives you a little more time to get your thoughts organized.
- **Breathe:** Deeply. It'll enhance your natural pitch and help your voice to become richer, fuller and stronger. Each new thought you express should be introduced with a new breath.
- **Enunciate:** Articulate yourself clearly and people will start seeing you as more confident, more intelligent and generally more capable.
- **Watch your tone:** Your tone of voice reflects the emotion behind your words and it can either amplify or detract from the words you choose to speak, so it is important to be aware of the emotions you are projecting. When you're talking through a problem, is your tone warm and understanding when it needs to be, or is it harsh and accusatory? People are wired to pick up on a whole plethora of cues, so make sure your tone, body language and facial expressions all reinforce the emotional meaning of your words.
- **Step away from the sarcasm:** When there's sarcasm around, somebody always gets burned.
- **Say it with a smile:** It's simple, but it works. A genuine, open smile can completely turn a conversation around.

The words you speak and the way you speak them can bring your ideas to life. They can help you create real connections with those around you. They can open doors. If you're not comfortable putting yourself out there, remember to give yourself permission to be there, wherever you are, whomever you're with. Give yourself permission to be valuable, and don't apologize. We have often observed women coming up with brilliant ideas whose expertise is just not recognized because of the way she puts it across. That's why it's vital to own what you say, even if it's not the best point in the room.

OWN HOW YOU SAY IT – NON VERBAL COMMUNICATION

Like it or not, the second you walk through the door, others will start sizing up your physical presence. How confidently do you walk in? How firmly do you shake hands? How are you holding yourself? In those first few moments, they're making decisions based on everything they observe.

So what exactly are you telling them?

If you're constantly fidgeting, pulling at your skirt, drumming your fingers, checking your phone, biting your nails, twirling your hair, tapping your pen...*stop*.

Be still. Breathe. And move with purpose.

If you're still debating about whether women should offer the limp wrist or a firm handshake, go with the firm handshake every time (unless you're in China where a lighter handshake is preferred). The handshake is much more than the hello of the business world; it's also an important gesture of trust and equality.

If you're slouching, hunching or making yourself small in any way, you're not going to project confidence. Even though physically shrinking might give you a sense of safety or comfort, don't do it. There's much more power in taking up space by standing tall. This has nothing to do with trying to be an "alpha" and everything to do with *feeling* more powerful.

If you want to own your physical space, you've got to come to terms with your own power. When we hear the word power, we sometimes associate it with negative connotations. But we have to change our mindset and realize that "power" is not a taboo word. Power doesn't have to be used to control others. It can be employed to raise everyone higher – including the organization as a whole.

Tom Peters (the 'Uber Guru' of business and personal branding who's written many best-selling leadership and management books, including *In Search of Excellence*) points out that "power for the most part is a badly misunderstood term and a badly misused capability." He contends that meaningful power is not measured by who has the biggest office or who has reached the highest point in the corporate hierarchy, but rather in who has influence or reputational power. "Power," Peters adds, "is largely a matter of perception. If you want people to see you as a powerful brand, act like a credible leader."

So how do you create that powerful persona? Here's one simple strategy: Volunteer to write the agenda for the next meeting and take the minutes, and then put your hand up to ensure that you are in charge of the action points following the meeting. Now you are effectively controlling the meeting and showing your leadership without being aggressive about it. You have put your hand up to take on a role, and nine times out of ten, people are happy to pass it on.

You could also try this mind trick when you are feeling intimidated: Imagine that you have just been crowned queen of the boardroom, and you walk into the room wearing a robe and a crown. You will find that your posture changes, because the robe is long as takes up space. That's the strategy branding specialist Koo Govender uses, and it works without fail to give her a secure knowledge of being in control of whatever is going to happen.

Govender also talks about living by the power of the "3 Ps." "I am completely *prepared*, and I am completely *present* in that meeting. When you're not prepared and you're not present, you lose that third P, your *power*. Being prepared means knowing your content and understanding it. Being present means being completely attentive to who and what's around you. I look at every person and try to understand how and what they are feeling. And I *listen*."

Because power and presence are so often equated with physical stature, women tend to struggle much more than their taller, broader, and often louder, male counterparts.

High-level strategic consultant at General Electric Julia Lazarus vividly remembers how she had to assert herself in order to own her presence. "Being female, looking young for my age, being only 5'3", and having a high-pitched voice, I had to work a little harder to earn credibility," she recalls. "When I was a General Manager running a $140-million business, I once had a customer ask me how long I had worked at my company. In other words, he wanted to know how young and inexperienced I was. I said, 'Take a guess, double it, and you'll be wrong.' He guessed twelve years when I had eighteen years of experience and was the most senior person in the room. His tone completely changed and he spent the rest of the meeting trying to make up for insulting me! Women have to be bold enough to do something like that to establish their credibility."

As women, we need to find our own ways to command our physical space and create a strong physical presence while retaining our femininity. We don't need to become men. We don't need to play the dominant alpha male. We don't need to emulate what our male counterparts are doing around us – like putting our hands behind our heads or our feet up on the desk in a display of dominance.

By moving the ribcage up, walking with purpose, standing tall, and sitting straight – like Govender does in the boardroom when she puts on her royal robe – we make ourselves more expansive and take up more of the space around us.

We can also become more expansive by using wide hand gestures to help illustrate a point. For example, if you're talking about a year-end report, use gestures to illustrate the increase in numbers. With one hand gesturing the lower number, raise your other hand above your head to illustrate the growth. This could seem pretty uncomfortable and awkward at first, but snap a picture of yourself doing this and you'll see that it doesn't look awkward at all. It looks assertive and expressive.

Direct eye contact is another way to affirm your presence and create strong connections with the people you're talking to. But always be respectful of the situation, your environment and the cultural differences of the people around you.

For example, in some cultures making eye contact is a sign of disrespect, so, if you sense that direct eye contact is making somebody feel uncomfortable, pull back. At the same time, if somebody avoids eye contact with you, don't just automatically dismiss that person as "untrustworthy." Consider that, in their culture, direct eye contact may be seen as disrespectful. Use your intuition – as women, many of us have an innate ability to read facial expressions and pick up on subtle emotional messages. Use this strength to your advantage.

What's more, it's not just other people who are influenced by our body language. Our own thoughts and feelings are influenced by the way we physically hold ourselves. Social psychologist Amy Cuddy has found that changing our posture for just two minutes can significantly change the way we feel about ourselves. People who spent just two minutes power posing (think Wonder Woman) before an interview increased their testosterone levels (the dominance hormone), decreased their cortisol levels (the stress hormone), created a far more compelling impression on the people who were assessing them and were ultimately evaluated higher overall than their peers who did the exact opposite of power posing. If you want to watch her TED Talk (it's fascinating!), here's the link: www.ted.com/talks/amy_cuddy_your_body_language_shapes_who_you_are.

Cuddy's work in this field demonstrates that our body language is not just relevant when it comes to perceptions of other people; it impacts how we feel about ourselves as well. When we strike a powerful pose, we're more likely to *feel* powerful.

Essentially, it comes down to this: your body can change your mind. Your mind changes your behavior. And your behavior changes your outcomes.

While recent research has questioned the scientific basis of some of Cuddy's assertions, we believe quite strongly in the power of self-awareness and body language. She is not actually telling us all to stand around striking the Wonder Woman pose during a meeting or presentation (thankfully). What she is saying, though, is that spending just a couple of private minutes being aware of our body language before we need to bring our absolute best to a particularly daunting situation can have an incredible impact on the way we feel and the physical presence we project.

EXERCISE: AMY CUDDY'S TWO-MINUTE POWER POSE

Before that big meeting, the public speech, the once-in-a-lifetime job interview, or that difficult phone conversation, close the door, give yourself two quiet minutes and hit a power pose. Our favorite is the Wonder Woman:

- Put your hands on your hips, stand with your feet wide apart, your shoulders back, and your chin up, and gaze confidently ahead.
- When you release your pose after two minutes, embrace the rising feelings of strength, composure and confidence within yourself and take them with you wherever it is you need to go.

Cuddy urges people to use this *absolutely free* tool as often as they need it. "Configure your brain to cope the best in those situations. Get your testosterone up, and get your cortisol down," she says. "This is not about faking it 'til you make it; it's about faking it 'til you *become* it."

OWN YOUR MEETINGS AND INTERVIEWS

They used to say that your co-workers assessed your competence, likability and trustworthiness in about seven seconds, but the latest research conducted by Harvard Medical School now suggests that all that happens in just 250 milliseconds! And that's all based simply on your appearance – so you really have to ensure you have it all worked out! Here are some tips on how to maximize your physical presence when it comes to meetings and interviews:

EYE CONTACT

This is something we touched on earlier, but in the context of a meeting or an interview, what matters is how quickly you make eye contact. Direct eye contact signals you are present and giving the other person your full attention. It also shows confidence and a willingness to connect.

GREETING

When you enter the boardroom, go up to each person, and introduce yourself to anyone you don't know. If it is a client you see regularly, greet each person individually. Always make an effort to acknowledge people and to treat them with the respect they deserve. If someone walked into a room and didn't bother to stand up or greet you, how would you feel?

Jennifer Dorian, the Senior Manager at Turner Classic Movies, says she used to come into a meeting room and grab a chair as quickly as possible. Her former boss and then CEO of Turner Networks, Steve Koonin, noticed this habit of hers. One day, as they were entering the boardroom, he suggested that she go over and talk to the gentleman who was conducting the meeting rather than grab her habitual chair. He also encouraged her to introduce herself and engage in some dialogue. She was then pleasantly surprised when, during the meeting, the meeting chair referred to something she had said to him. Dorian recalls that as a turning point in her life. When she mentors others, she refers to it as claiming your space in the pre-game. You see, owning your physical space is not only important when you are giving a presentation or conducting a meeting; it is also your ability to walk into a room with a smile and with the confidence to talk to anyone.

Let's take this one step back. When your client walks in to collect you for the meeting in their reception area, they don't want to greet the top of your head buried in your phone or your tablet. There's nothing wrong with catching up on emails or reading if you are early, but when it's time for the person to arrive, put the devices away. When they actually walk in, you will be ready to greet them, and the first impression will be a positive one.

Make sure you have enough business cards with you, and more importantly, keep them in an easy-to-access place like the front of your notebook, a card carrier, or a specific place in your bag. Do not scrounge around in your bag looking for the last card that is bent and stained with lipstick. This is what they have to remember you by.

PREPARATION

As Govender said, preparation is critical to a successful meeting. But preparation isn't just about preparing the work. Have you ever thought to research who you are presenting to or being interviewed by? Look over their LinkedIn profile, and read some of their tweets or blog posts if available. When chatting in your meeting, use your knowledge to show them you have taken the time to research them and planned appropriately. You can say something like, "I really enjoyed your article on X, have you ever read [this author]?" Or, "I saw a few of your tweets and I think you would find this site really interesting." It is not sucking up or coming across as inauthentic. Quite the contrary. It is actually forming a genuine connection.

MINDSET

When you walk into a boardroom or an interview, act as if you are the host. Don't think of yourself as the subject because that immediately reduces you to a submissive position. That said, do not go the other extreme and walk in with an air of arrogance. You want to come off as self-assured. When you enter the room, smile, be friendly and use a firm handshake. If you are being interviewed, don't forget that an interview is a two-way street and you are also interviewing your prospective employer. Do not give away your power and never be afraid to ask questions.

BODY LANGUAGE

We suggest that you re-read the section on non-verbal body language. Slouching and being distracted on your phone in a meeting says something about your engagement with the meeting, or even your role. Rather, maintain an upright posture, shoulders pulled back, and when you sit, cross your legs and keep your arms at your sides. Be physically present so that you send out signals that are congruent with what you do.

PARTICIPATION

One of the main criticisms women face is that they often don't speak up in meetings. Sometimes it's fear, sometimes it's for cultural reasons. But the corporate landscape is changing, and, more and more, women are making their mark in the boardroom. Meetings and interviews are great opportunities to show off your knowledge and voice your opinion...so you have to say *something*! The reality is, if you don't make yourself heard, no one will know your value. This is how you really own your physical space.

PUNCTUALITY

This may seem like a given, but if someone is waiting for you to arrive and you're late, it detracts from your presence. It shows a lack of respect for the other person's time. Plan ahead. Do you have the directions? Do you know the correct floor and suite number? Do you know where to park? Have you considered the time of day of your meeting? What's the traffic like? Security is another huge time-waster. We strongly advise leaving at least ten minutes extra for signing in with security, especially if you need to check in your laptop or tablet. If your meeting is at 10 am, you cannot arrive at 10 am. You need to make sure you are sitting in reception, already signed in and ready for them to collect you. When it's a first-time meeting at a restaurant or coffee shop, always ensure you have the phone number of the person you are meeting and text them on arrival to say where you are sitting and what you are wearing. This prevents any uncomfortable situations. Another bit of advice is to arrive earlier to secure the table if you know it is a busy place. When the other person arrives, there is no delay and you can begin your meeting at the scheduled time. Always be conscious of the other person's time; if it is someone very senior, their time is always limited and you want to maximize the time booked with them to discuss your agenda, not to wait around to be seated. If you invited the person to the meeting, then you must offer to pay the bill. It can really derail their perception of you if you expect them to pay.

PRESENTATIONS

If you are presenting to a client and need to use a laptop to show a video or PowerPoint presentation, give yourself time to check it first. Make sure you test it before you arrive. We always recommend arriving a bit early to test the equipment as well, especially if you have video or sound clips built into your presentation. Another rule of thumb is to always have a backup on a flash drive in case your equipment decides to go on strike. And, just to be on the safe side, have a printed version of your presentation. That way, if you've tested everything before the group arrives, you can relax and just focus on the task at hand. That is much preferable to the frazzled feeling of having the group sitting around the table waiting for you to boot up the computer and open your files.

Arriving early and prepared leaves an impression of being organized and in control, and these are traits anyone will want to see in someone they're doing business with. If you are in an industry that requires a presentation that is not digital, such as physical drawings or papers, ensure you arrive with them in a suitably-sized carrier bag and that you have the papers or materials organized in the order you would like to present them. Nothing will undermine your credibility and presence more than a disorganized presentation that features papers flying around the room!

OWN YOUR CHARISMA

We've outlined the recipe for owning your physical space through your attire, as well as verbal and non-verbal behaviors, but what really connects these three aspects of physical presence is charisma. How often do we look in awe at people like Richard Branson or Michelle Obama because they have a trait that is so alluring? They have charisma. And they radiate this energy and confidence with absolute ease whenever they walk into a room.

So, what exactly is "charisma"? It's that quality that says, "Hello, I am comfortable with myself; I am confident; I own my space."

Olivia Fox Cabane, author of *The Charisma Myth*, believes that people aren't born with charisma, no matter how magnetic they may appear. "No one is charismatic twenty-four hours a day," she writes. "This is because charisma is not some kind of magical aura, but the result of certain learnable behaviors."

These behaviors include both what we say and do, and how we say and do it. Do we come across as being as comfortable and as confident as we can be?

Charismatic people often exude the perception that they have discovered a sense of joy about the world and they are willing to share it. The good news is there is no single way of projecting charisma. More reserved people can be magnetic, whereas those of us who are more extroverted can be more dynamic.

According to Cabane, there are several charisma styles, and the key is to find the right one for you. Not all people are charismatic in the same way, and different situations require different kinds of charisma. Among the distinct charisma styles she has identified are the following:

- *Focus charisma* lets people know you're fully present, as exemplified by former president Bill Clinton.
- *Visionary charisma* inspires people or gets them to believe in something in the way Nelson Mandela was able to transform South Africa.
- *Kindness charisma,* as shown by Mother Theresa, makes others feel seen and accepted.
- *Authority charisma* makes others believe you have the power to change their lives. For some people, President Barack Obama has this quality, while others might be swayed by other political candidates with different views.

How do you choose the right one? This depends on your personality, your goals and the situation. When choosing a style, remain consistent with your personality. In terms of goals, think about how you want people to respond to you. You can adapt styles to the situation by combining or alternating between them. Denise Restauri, founder and CEO of GirlQuake™ and a *Forbes* contributor, provides some important qualities of a charismatic person, divided into presence, body language and verbal communication:

PHYSICAL PRESENCE AND BODY LANGUAGE:
- **Be fully present:** This is a skill that makes you stand out but is often hard to achieve. The trick is to give people your full attention. Although many people seem to think that taking the occasional peek at their phone won't be noticed, it absolutely will. People can sense whether or not they are getting your full attention.

- **Be self-confident:** Be comfortable with who you are. Be consistent. Hold your own.
- **Body-speak:** Be open and approachable, gracious and graceful. How do you do that? The answer is to own the room when you walk into it.

VERBAL COMMUNICATION

- **Speak with conviction:** Don't get bombastic, but try to use strong phrases like *I am sure* rather than more tentative phrases like *I think, I hope* and *I feel*.
- **Tell great stories:** We all love a good story, and it's a great way to begin a presentation, keep people's attention, and present a powerful idea.
- **Be relevant:** Know what's happening in the world and around you. People want to be with people who are in-the-know.
- **Be a good listener:** You can't remember everything, but remembering someone's name is a big deal. Here's a trick: when you are introduced to a person, immediately repeat their name. Example: "Amanda, it's so nice to meet you."
- **Make the conversation about the other person:** Let the world revolve around the person you're talking to. Give them your undivided attention. Immediately put others at ease and make them feel comfortable with you.

OWN YOUR PHYSICAL SPACE...IN A FLASH

- Conduct a personal-presence audit: What does your current appearance and behavior portray about you?
- Be authentic.
- Dress for the job you want, not the job you have.
- Give your wardrobe the SPF test (structure, proportion and fit).
- Expand into the space around you: walk tall, stand tall, sit straight. Wear your robe.
- Own what you say verbally.
- Listen.
- Speak from the heart.
- Own what you say non-verbally.
- Move with purpose.
- Power-pose for two minutes to increase your feelings of inner confidence whenever you need it most.
- Own your meetings and interviews.
- Develop your own personal style of charisma.

3 Own
YOUR PEOPLE SKILLS

People will forget what you said, will forget what you did, but people will never forget how you made them feel.

— MAYA ANGELOU

We may be able to choose our friends, but we're not always in control of who our colleagues or bosses are. In fact, it's quite likely that we'll find ourselves working with people we don't always gel with, or even with people we don't like very much. In a group of people large enough, it's almost guaranteed that there'll be one we clash with in one way or another. But when someone at work behaves in a way that upsets or hurts us, walking away in the hopes that we'll never have to deal with them again is definitely not the answer.

Neither, of course, as much as we may feel like doing it, is yelling, screaming, rolling our eyes, or pounding our fists. The open expression of a negative emotion can make a bad situation much, much worse – and, let's face it, it is just not acceptable. But because we are human, there *are* going to be negative emotions at the workplace – emotions that can be further inflamed by complex personalities. It's all part of what makes handling and defusing conflict so immensely challenging.

Our interpersonal or people skills come down to how well we interact with the people around us, and the strength of the relationships that we build. We already know that performance alone doesn't count for everything. Of course our ability to do our jobs well is critical to our career success, but often it's our overall *image* that plays a bigger role in determining how successful we will be. And central to that image is how we handle our interpersonal relationships.

Most of the time we're so busy chasing deadlines, managing relentlessly growing piles of work, and dealing with the daily demands of our over-connected lives, that we're not always in tune with our emotions. We react without thinking. When the pressure is on, when the stakes are high, and the expectations are even higher, those instinctive reactions may not be the ones that work in our favor.

The key here is not to react when you're not in full control of your emotions. In our conversations with business leaders and human resource professionals all over the world, we keep hearing the same thing over and over: There is no one factor that sabotages a career more than an individual's inability to handle conflict skillfully.

During the course of your career, there is no doubt that at some point you will have to deal with a challenging situation or individual. It is inevitable that there will be differences of opinion. Donnell King, an Associate Professor of Speech and Journalism at Pellissippi State Community College, says that "interpersonal communication is inescapable, irreversible, complex and contextual. It's inescapable because we're dealing with other people, irreversible because we cannot take back what we say, complex because things get lost in translation, and contextual because when and where you speak will impact the meaning of your message and how it is received." One of our favorite sayings is "In the absence of proper information, people come to their own conclusions. Factors such as gender, personality, and cultural differences can play a major role in interpreting what is being said."

While skilled interpersonal communication takes concerted effort and conscientiousness, remember that we always have a choice. We can either choose to be part of the problem or part of the solution. It is much more positive to build your reputation as a problem-solver than as a problem-builder. In essence, it is much more constructive to strive to become part of the solution, because by doing that, we defuse the conflict, find a practical solution, and maintain self-respect.

Become the kind of person everyone else wants to work with. When we raise our level of emotional intelligence, when we begin to understand our own personality style and those of the people we interact with, when we listen actively and develop strategies to deal with difficult individuals and situations, we start relating to others in the most effective, powerful and gracious way.

Own Your EQ

So what exactly is emotional intelligence? Simply put, emotional intelligence (also known as EQ or EI) is a combination of five factors. The first three have to do with your relationship with yourself: self-awareness, self-regulation and motivation. The other two have to do with your relationship toward others: empathy and social skills. Daniel Goleman, the authority on EQ, lists the five factors as self-awareness, self-regulation, motivation, empathy, and social skills.

SELF-AWARENESS

Self-awareness is simply that. How aware are you of yourself, your moods, your emotions, your triggers, your responses, and how these impact other people? People with an evolved sense of self-awareness are generally self-confident and have a realistic assessment of themselves, their thoughts and their behaviors. They don't take themselves too seriously, and they aren't overly judgmental.

SELF-REGULATION

Self-regulation is the ability to control or redirect negative and impulsive actions or emotions by rising above petty arguments, jealousies and frustrations. A person who has a high level of self-regulation thinks before acting and refrains from making impulsive decisions. People with a strong sense of self-regulation are usually trustworthy and have a high degree of integrity; they are open to change and willing to accept the discomfort of ambiguity and uncertainty.

MOTIVATION

How excited are you about what you're doing? How driven are you to do the very best you can at every given opportunity? What is your incentive? There are two types of motivation: internal and external. Your passion and enthusiasm for your work is your internal motivation. Position, status and income are all external motivations. We have found that internally motivated people are driven by energy and fulfillment in their work. They pursue goals with persistence; they love a challenge and, generally speaking, these individuals are highly productive. Motivated leaders and employees have a strong desire to achieve and if they have to, they'll defer immediate results for long-term success. They're optimistic and can easily move past failure and frustration. These kinds of people are inspiring and motivating. Having heard this description, would you consider yourself as someone who is motivated?

EMPATHY

Think of the last time somebody told you about their unfortunate circumstances and you almost tangibly felt their pain. Did you tear up when they did? That ability to relate with and experience someone else's emotional state is empathy. People who are empathetic treat others with respect, kindness and professionalism. They identify with and understand the feelings, wants, needs and viewpoints of those around them. They don't stereotype and they don't judge. They listen, and they listen well. Empathetic leaders are often naturally skilled at choosing and retaining employees.

SOCIAL SKILLS

How would you rate your social skills? Are you comfortable engaging in conversations with others? Are you comfortable initiating conversations, or do you find yourself waiting until you are spoken to? Good social skills in the workplace put you in a more powerful position to manage relationships and build networks. People with strong social skills are excellent communicators, are persuasive, are effective at initiating change, and know how to build and lead teams. These people don't always put their own needs ahead of the team's needs – they're team players who want to see others shine.

•••

Goleman's research shows that the higher up you get in an organization, the more your success depends on your emotional versus intellectual intelligence. Time and time again, we see that people who have an ability to understand their own emotional wellbeing and that of others are happier and more successful.

Being in touch with our emotions (which as women we often are) can be a great asset because our emotions can be indispensable in pushing us to take action. It's something that we should embrace, but we should also take care that they do not derail us.

So, how can we use the power of our emotions constructively without allowing them to overwhelm us? According to Goleman, that's where emotional *intelligence* comes into play. He says EQ allows us to recognize and manage our feelings without being controlled by them. A large part of our ability to navigate the workplace successfully depends on our ability to read other people's signals and to react to them appropriately.

Goleman discovered that although the qualities commonly associated with leadership (like intelligence, decisiveness, determination and vision) are necessary for success, they aren't enough. Highly effective leaders also have a solid degree of emotional intelligence. In fact, Goleman reveals direct links between a leader's emotional intelligence and measurable business results.

But EQ isn't just important for leaders. It's something we all need every day. Research has demonstrated that a stronger EQ translates to greater levels of happiness in general, better mental and physical health, improved relationships, and a decrease in levels of the stress hormone cortisol. Moreover, in order to progress to your next career goal, whether you're aiming for a promotion, growing your business, or even just wanting more successful and harmonious relationships, emotional intelligence is critical. Julia Lazarus confirms that emotional intelligence has been the biggest career accelerator for her because it helped her know how to read people and situations, and, just as important, to know "which battles to fight and which ones aren't worth it."

If you're worried that you might not be scoring very high in the EQ department, here's the good news: you can develop it. Drawing from Goleman's five components of EQ, and inspired by her own work in the field, clinical psychologist Dr. Colinda Linde shares a few steps we can all take to boost our EQ levels:

OWN YOUR SELF-AWARENESS

- Start noticing how you feel throughout the day.
- Become cognizant of the source of your emotions.
- Notice what triggers certain emotions.
- Actively remember that emotions are fleeting and should not be the foundation of your decision-making.
- Acknowledge the repercussions of your behavior. Realize that your negative emotions in the past have probably had an undesirable effect on the people around you.
- Ask for feedback. Look at your past performance reviews and get feedback from your boss and colleagues you trust.
- Take an honest look at yourself. What are your strengths and weaknesses? Enhance your strengths and actively work on improving your weak areas.
- Think ahead. Plan ways to manage your emotions so that you're not caught off-guard next time.

As one of our clients who has worked in HR in the corporate world for 25 years says, "Nobody comes to the office with an intention to offend or be difficult, to be autocratic, aggressive or to cause conflict, and yet we all have witnessed that type of behavior. The number one cause is simply a lack of self-awareness."

OWN YOUR SELF-REGULATION

- Wait. In potentially inflammatory situations, make it a habit to press your internal pause button and give it a few hours or days before responding. It will give you a chance to cool off and think straight.
- Stay away from office politics, drama or conflict. You might want to be part of the group, but it could undermine your integrity and professional behavior.
- Accept that uncertainty, frustrations and disappointments are part of the work environment.
- Brainstorm solutions instead of complaining or acting out. Present those solutions calmly and professionally.
- Distract yourself. If someone's annoying you in a meeting, give your mind something else to hang on to rather than responding impulsively. You can distract yourself from the negative emotion for a while by spelling a word backwards in your head or counting back in sevens from an obscure number like 312.

- Don't allow stress to compromise your EQ and integrity. Consistently release and manage stress outside of work. Try exercise, meditation, creative hobbies, or simply spending time with friends and family.

- Remember when you are responding to something out of anger, irritation or fear, that the sane, rational part of your brain is hijacked. Goleman describes this as Amygdala Hijack, more commonly known as flight or fight syndrome. The blood flows to your extremities rather than the brain, where you most need it for rational thinking. You need to be in control and yet often you aren't.

The ability to check in with yourself and hold an internal dialogue is critical to your being able to question what's really happening around you. Don't just accept a feeling. Sometimes that emotion doesn't serve you well. With internal dialogue, you can change your perception of what's going on. Ask yourself what is real, what is not, and whether you are handling it in the best possible way.

OWN YOUR MOTIVATION

We all have periods when our motivation fluctuates. Brand guru Melissa Dawn Simkins says that the people who succeed are the ones with internal motivation. They don't need approval from others. Here are ways to keep your inner motivation more consistent:

- Find what you love. Identify all those things you love about your job and the reason you find your job so fulfilling. Don't obsess about the parts of your job that you don't like; rather focus your attention on the parts that you do, and brainstorm ways to spend more time on what inspires you.

- Practice optimism. This may sound trite and obvious, but you can improve your ability to respond if you are optimistic. Your level of optimism is often very tangible in your vocal inflection, facial expression and the level of enthusiasm with which you communicate.

- Thought-replace. You can improve your level of optimism by catching yourself whenever you speak or think negatively, and consciously reframing your thoughts and words. When you find yourself caught up in a negative spiral of thinking, shout out to yourself, "Stop!" While allowing the negative, unhelpful thought to arise and move on, you can redirect your attention toward a more helpful thought.

- Set inspiring goals for yourself. Determine specific actions to reach your goals, and reward yourself for every milestone and accomplishment along the way.

Set achievable goals. For example, if you want to get into shape, walk for 30 minutes, three times a week. If you want to raise your profile, write a regular thought leadership piece on LinkedIn.

- Recognize that others are drawn to positive, energized and inspiring people. As you improve your motivation, you'll see that you get more attention from decision-makers, clients and peers.

OWN YOUR EMPATHY

Most people do have the ability to empathize with others on some level. To improve on this, here are some additional tools:

- Make a conscious and concerted effort to view the situation from the other person's point of view, especially in a conflict situation.
- Validate their point of view. Don't just see it; let them know that you understand where they're coming from and that their perspective has merit.
- Instead of judging someone as right or wrong, or good or bad, recognize that they're working from the knowledge and experience they have.
- Examine your own attitude and motives. Do you just want to be right to prove a point or win the argument, or are you truly interested in the best outcome or solution?
- Listen. Actively. Take it all in and reflect back what the other person is saying so it's clear that you both understand what's being communicated. When people feel heard, they tend to be more willing to cooperate and compromise.

OWN YOUR SOCIAL SKILLS

- Be a better communicator. Listen carefully. Ask thoughtful questions. Be clear and accurate in providing information. Sharpen your writing skills.
- Analyze the non-verbal signs. Learn how to judge someone's mood just by looking at cues, like their facial expressions and their body language.
- Learn the elegant art of persuasion. Make real connections with people; use solid knowledge and sound reasoning for your point of view, and let your passion shine through.
- Become the go-to person. When you have integrity, when you're even- handed and calm, and you're committed to finding the best outcome, people will begin to see you as essential and knowledgeable.

- Understand the person you're talking to. You can't have a one-size-fits-all approach to interacting with everyone in the workplace. Learn how to finesse and tailor your interactions with other people based on their personality, cultural orientation and position within the company.

OWN YOUR PERSONALITY STYLE

A key factor in developing a higher level of emotional intelligence is the ability to see the world from another person's point of view. This often starts with understanding that they may have a different personality style and a different way of looking at things than you do. It's an attitude that Arlette Guthrie, often brings to her position as the non-store Human Resources Vice President at The Home Depot. "Throughout my career it has served me well to recognize that there will be all kinds of personalities in the room. People will have all kinds of different perspectives and points of view from whatever their experiences may be. Be prepared that the conversation can go in any direction, but be open, because there is no one best way to do anything."

Dr. Tony Alessandra, a seasoned marketing guru, has identified four basic personality styles: Directors, Socializers, Relaters, and Thinkers. The Director, for example, is results-orientated, decisive and direct, while the Thinker is careful, detailed and reserved. The Relater is likely to be friendly and avoid conflict, while the Socializer is enthusiastic and creative.

Alessandra points out that it is only by understanding the nuances through which other individuals see the world that we can begin to relate to them in a meaningful way. When you treat people the way *you* want to be treated, you actually create relationship tension. When you treat people the way *they* want to be treated, you build rapport.

Your ability to build rapport and to relate to as many different personality styles as possible is one of the most valuable qualities you can possess. To do this, it is important to learn how to read your colleagues' verbal, vocal (voice inflection) and visual signals, and then to adapt your behavior in order to accommodate their behavioral styles. According to Alessandra, there are a range of strategies to communicate effectively with people of different personalities, particularly in the case of conflict situations:

DEALING WITH THE DIRECTOR

When communicating with a Director personality type, focus on results, give direct answers and lower your expectations for an empathetic response to your particular issue.

DEALING WITH THE THINKER

The Thinker prefers to be given as many details as possible. They appreciate time to gather information and decide on solutions. In a conflict situation, this person will need time to reflect on or digest the issue at hand before responding.

DEALING WITH THE SOCIALIZER

The Socializer is a creative, rather than a detail person, who appreciates the freedom to plan and accomplish their work.

DEALING WITH THE RELATOR

As the warm and friendly personality type who is most likely to avoid conflict, the Relater values expressions of appreciation and support.

PUTTING IT ALL INTO ACTION

The more open person usually enjoys personal interaction that is warm and lively and, in the case of conflicts and disagreements, will probably be more receptive to honest discussions of the issue. On the other hand, a more reserved individual is likely to shut down and head for the hills if approached too quickly when conflicts arise. This kind of individual will need time to think over the issue, and would probably respond well to a low-key, non-confrontational effort to solve the problem at hand.

While the Socializer would probably respond positively to a face-to-face discussion of a contentious issue in a conflict situation, a more reserved individual like the Thinker is likely to be more comfortable if you communicate with him or her by email or text. People who have strong Director qualities usually appreciate direct, results-oriented communication, and the creative personality types often respond well to communication that refers to their field of interest.

Some people value interpersonal relationships, while others are more comfortable as loners. A person who is invested in interpersonal relationships may value expressions of appreciation and support, and are relatively comfortable dealing with interpersonal conflicts and disagreements. A loner or an introverted, detail-oriented individual is not likely to respond well to over-enthusiastic behavior that they feel is impinging on their personal space, and may prefer a certain distance. A colleague or ours who managed a high-profile radio station, told us how she works with a wide range of personalities. "I manage people based on their temperaments," Alessandra says. "The way I would manage an on-air personality is different to the way I would manage a technician who is quiet and more reserved. There are so many big personalities at the station, but understanding personal boundaries makes it easy."

UNDERSTAND THE POWER OF LISTENING

Developing a greater understanding of both yourself and others is a main factor in truly owning your interpersonal space. There is no better way to show your improvement than by becoming a better listener, and when applied consistently this skill is extremely powerful.

In our careers, it's critical that we are heard. But it's just as critical that we hear – that we *truly* hear. Think about it: we often appear to be listening but in fact we are so distracted by other thoughts, other people, and other things we have to do, that we're not really actively listening. Or we're thinking about what we're going to say next and how we can say it so that we sound fabulously articulate and intelligent. We don't entirely hear what the person in front of us is saying. We're not getting the whole message.

Our ability to really listen to others is as vital to our overall presence as every other aspect covered in this book. When we actively listen, we're in a better position to get the whole story. We hear what is being said, how it's being said, and often more importantly, what isn't being said. We start to see the whole picture, we grow in understanding and we learn. In the wise words of talk show legend Larry King, "I never learned anything while I was talking."

The more we listen, the more people tend to share, because ultimately people have a need to be heard. To remain unheard is almost like being invisible. When you give people the respect of listening to what they have to say and you value their right to express themselves, you make them feel more valuable. Don't ever underestimate the power of giving someone the opportunity to be listened to.

Apart from making people feel valuable in your presence, active listening broadens your world in so many other ways. You gain new information, see different perspectives, spot problems before they become issues, and become inspired by other people. In more ways than one, active listening is the path to greater creativity, smarter innovations and higher levels of productivity.

One way to create strong interpersonal communication skills and become a better listener is to "be Switzerland." Leadership coach Marshall Goldsmith suggests that, for a week, you think of yourself as a human Switzerland. That means that any idea that comes your way from another person is treated with complete neutrality. Don't take sides, don't express an opinion and don't judge the comment. Just say, "Thank you." Or even, "Thanks, I hadn't considered that." Or, "Thanks. You've given me something to think about." After one week, Goldsmith guarantees you'll have significantly reduced the number of pointless arguments you engage in at work or at home.

According to Goldsmith, nobody can argue with you when you don't judge their ideas. "People will gradually begin to see you as much more agreeable, even when you are not in fact agreeing with them," he says. "Do this consistently and people will eventually perceive you as a welcoming person, someone whose door they can knock on when they have an idea, someone they can brainstorm with and not feel demotivated or judged."

One of our clients decided to put this into practice, not just for one week, but for the entire duration of her third trimester of pregnancy. Up until then, she had been worn down on a daily basis by well-meaning colleagues who were constantly dishing out "expert advice" about childbirth and pregnancy. She decided to bank the ideas that worked for her, and discard the ones that didn't. But whether the advice was good or bad, she'd smile graciously and say, "Thank you." She understood that all people wanted to do was help her, and she acknowledged it without judgment. It made her life a whole lot easier from then on.

Of course, there's much more to skillful listening than being a "human Switzerland." Skillful listening is a highly active process, but at least it's not a complicated one. It's just a matter of breaking some old bad habits, becoming more conscious and putting healthy new skills into place.

Here is a great listening exercise that is worth practicing. We use this in our workshops, and, long past their training, people tell us it's an incredibly memorable and useful tool. Start by dividing people into groups of two where one person shares their greatest challenge. The person listening cannot interject with their own experience, but rather has to focus on the other person and cannot bring it back to his or her own issues. This exercise will definitely increase your awareness of how we tend to want to focus on ourselves and teaches us to be truly present.

FINE TUNE YOUR LISTENING SKILLS

- **Prepare yourself to listen:** Stop what you're doing, put down that phone, put away auditory and visual distractions, hush your thoughts, and, most of all, stop talking. Listening is an active process, so it requires your absolute attention.
- **Show that you're ready to listen:** Make eye contact, focus on the speaker, and if you are sitting across from them, lean forward. Don't fold your arms. Use your body language to make the speaker feel relaxed enough to speak freely.
- **Listen closely:** Focus on what is being said. Now is not the time to plan a response, formulate an opinion or solve a problem. Now is the time to listen. Simply allow this person to express themselves and allow their views to be heard.
- **Be respectful:** Don't judge, don't bring your personal prejudices into play and don't censor what somebody else is trying to say. Practice curiosity instead. Open your mind and be respectful of the story unfolding in front of you.
- **Listen deeply:** Listen as much to the things that *aren't* being said as the things that *are* being said. Pay attention to the tone of voice, be mindful of the words that are chosen and watch the speaker's body language.
- **Be patient:** Don't jump in. Even when the speaker pauses, fumbles for the right words, or stutters, don't finish his or her sentences and don't interrupt.
- **Understand:** When the full story is on the table, make sure you get it with absolute clarity. Ask questions if you have to. Paraphrase it back to the speaker. Get all the details you need, not later, *now*.
- **And when you do respond:** Think first, self-evaluate and ask yourself, "Is what I am about to say going to make a valuable contribution?"

It feels good to be heard; it feels even better to be understood. And if you're the one who can give that to the people around you, you grow your own potential to create stronger, healthier, more solid relationships.

However much you understand other people's personality styles and truly listen to their issues, it is still inevitable that you will disagree with their point of view at some stage. Some of us see this as disagreement, some as conflict and others as outright war.

Which are you? And how good are you at dealing with day-to-day conflict?

As we said earlier, your ability to resolve conflict well is an essential part of a positive image. Conversely, your inability to handle conflict can be very damaging.

UNDERSTAND HOW TO RESOLVE CONFLICT

Conflict. That uncomfortable place. For some it's utterly terrifying. Even just the word can be enough to stir ripples of anxiety, and some people will do anything to shy away from it. The reality is that conflict is a natural part of life; it's something we all have to deal with frequently. But is it all that bad?

Because conflict arises when one person's ideas, concerns or desires differ from those of another, it's almost entirely unavoidable. Yes, for some of us, it's an uncomfortable place to be; yes, it can be a negative experience, but conflict can also be a positive force. Depending on how skillfully and creatively you manage conflict, you can come out the other side with greater self-confidence, a boost in productivity, and grand leaps in innovation.

So when you find yourself faced with conflict, whether it's a nasty person or an offensive email, the first step is to take a step backwards. Don't react immediately. Do yourself (and everybody around you) a big favor: employ that tried-and-tested, calming measure of taking a deep breath. And another. Count to ten if you can. Picture a tranquil ocean scene if you need to. Give yourself some time to think straight. Just don't go off on a negative rant because you might say something you'll regret or send an email that'll hover around in cyberspace forever. You're not going to look very professional. You might actually even lose credibility. And it's not going to do anybody any good.

If you can wait a little before responding, wait. An hour. A day, if you can. Even better, give yourself the night to sleep on it. That way you can create a healthier distance between your emotions and the issue; you can clear your thoughts on how you want to approach the issue and you get a little time to practice the conversation that you have to have.

Just don't wait forever.

Conflicts that are not addressed are likely to fester and can cause long-term problems. Even if you try to brush it off and forget about it, it'll be hovering around in your subconscious. If you don't face the things that bother you, there'll come a time when something will set you off. And suddenly your unresolved issue from the past is far bigger than it ever should have been.

Indeed, one of our colleagues believes that shying away from conflict is extremely counter-productive. "Conflict management takes some time to perfect," she says. "If something is not working, step away, cool off, think again, get your headspace right, and come back with a better approach. People use the excuse of a personality clash but the reality is that we cannot like everyone, and that does not mean we cannot work together. There is always a solution, always."

Dealing with conflict effectively begins with honesty. And the first person you've got to be honest with is yourself, because sometimes the most difficult person to deal with in a conflict is yourself. If there is a constant stream of conflict in your life, whether it's at work, at home, or both, you need to take a careful look in the mirror. Are you the common denominator? Could it be your thoughts, beliefs, attitudes or responses that are the source of the conflict and tension you keep experiencing in your life? It may even be something as simple as your body language. Whatever it is, for the sake of your career, it's important to be open to the possibility that the source of your conflicts may stem from something you're doing (or not doing).

As much as there are different styles of personalities, there are different ways of dealing with conflict. Some people bully their way through and always have to be right. To the other extreme, some people are people-pleasers, always giving in to make the other person right. In the book *Crucial Conversations*, authors Kerry Patterson, Joseph Grenny, Ron McMillan, and Al Switzler refer to these two styles as "silence versus violence." Our suggestion is that you try to find a balance between the two. When dealing with conflict, always go in asking yourself, *What is my intent?* For example, if you're having a conflict with a co-worker, your intent could be to maintain a cooperative, friendly relationship. In that case, the first step is to let them know what has made you upset. Be very factual about it. Then, instead of blaming and shaming, ask your co-worker to share his or her response with you. Nobody can argue with a solution that benefits both parties, so collaboration is truly the ideal to aspire to.

An extremely useful strategy is to strive to live by the tenet of assuming positive intent. Instead of flaring up in anger or making an assumption about where the other person is coming from, take a moment to consider the situation from their perspective. Then proceed from the assumption that this individual really intends to do the right thing. You'll probably find that the person who is causing you distress is actually surprised by your conciliatory attitude.

"You don't have to scream and shout, especially not in front of other people," says veteran event organizer Edith Venter. "Rather, take the individual aside and let them understand how you feel and also how they feel. If I get an email that accuses me of something, I will always sleep on it and reply the next day. The tone is better and I'm calmer. When you react on emotions, it creates a mess and you can never take it back."

In a conflict situation, most people expect an aggressive response because they're ready to fight. So try responding with: "I'm sorry, there seems to be some misunderstanding here...Help me understand – how can we resolve this?" You'll be amazed by the reaction. You could even try this powerful question: "Can you tell me a little more about what's behind this?" Now, you are the one who has made a conscious choice to seek constructive solutions, rather than to win a war.

As human beings, we instinctively defend ourselves, and if we perceive that we are being attacked, we assume the worst and our defense can be quite aggressive. A conciliatory attitude may seem to be counterintuitive because it goes against our primal instinct to defend ourselves, but keep in mind that this is not "wimping out." You're not responding from a position of weakness. Quite the opposite, in fact – you will be responding from a position of strength.

Of course, there is always an alternative. And that alternative is to stay in a mode of conflict. The potential damage, however, is that you may be viewed as less productive, less polished and less accomplished than you really are. You always have a choice. And if you make the conscious choice to seek constructive solutions, the war you will be winning is of your reputation and credibility. You'll be seen as an effective collaborator and a problem-solver – and that is immensely powerful in the overall trajectory of your life and career.

Conflict management is also about timing. If you need to resolve a conflict, or if you sense that a conflict is brewing, be selective about the timing of your conversation. When the person you need to have that conversation with is stressed out, in a foul mood, distracted, or rushing out the door to make a meeting, it's not the right time to engage in conversation. You're not going to get the best out of him or her. What you might get, however, is a touchy response. Things have a much better chance of working out when you find some time that works for both of you. When you're both a little calmer and more relaxed, schedule it into your calendar so that you can deal with it appropriately.

When you finally have their full attention, remember that the way you start the conversation is critical. Defensiveness is the enemy of collaboration. You'll have little chance of a collaborative resolution if the person you're talking to feels under attack. Be neutral. Neutrality allows for a mature, open and honest discussion.

We suggest starting the conversation by saying something like, "I would like to chat to you about what happened yesterday. I don't feel like we are on the same page." Or you could try, "I think there was a misunderstanding between us, do you have some time to chat about it?" When you approach people in a neutral way, they're not as likely to feel like they're under interrogation and they'll be more open to the discussion.

While you're working on keeping your cool, you'll find it extremely helpful to develop the ability to see the world from the other person's point of view. Not only do we see things differently because of our different backgrounds – our different cultures, religions and philosophies – but, as we discussed previously, we also have different personalities. That means that we're not all going to handle situations in the same way. It also means that we're not all going to get along.

Most of us choose to connect with people who have a disposition similar to our own. But because we don't necessarily get to choose who our work colleagues are, we might find that their personality styles are very different to ours. An extrovert may find it challenging to negotiate with quieter, more reserved people. To a more sociable and people-orientated person, a co-worker who is totally focused on work and on getting the job done may at first appear cold and uninterested in the emotional dimensions of an issue.

We all relate to people differently depending on our own personality styles. Some of us are very open and share personal details quickly. Some of us are more reserved and would never think of discussing our personal lives at a first meeting. There are those people who leave a meeting having noticed the tension that existed between two colleagues, and there are those so focused on the task at hand that they didn't notice any tension at all.

Although it may not always be very obvious to you, the differences in personality styles can be as vast and divisive as differences in age, background and culture. Developing emotional intelligence is important for both your survival and your success in any environment.

EXERCISE: UNDERSTAND HOW YOU HANDLE CONFLICT

Take a close look at yourself by asking:

- Do I understand my personality style?
- Do I respond defensively to criticism?
- Do I have a constant need to be right?
- Am I always in a hurry to get the job done?
- Do I find it difficult to wait while other people catch up with my understanding and the approach I would like to take?
- Is it always someone else's fault?

Conflict resolution is rarely clear-cut or black and white. In fact, there are more and more gray areas as the workplace becomes more generationally and culturally diverse than ever before. Respect these differences. Instead of imposing your hierarchy or rank, value the unique differences in people and learn to see things from differing points of view so that you can understand how to avoid conflict better in the future.

When you develop the interpersonal skills to keep your cool and handle difficult interpersonal situations with grace and with power, you will have met one of the most important challenges of attaining a professional presence. Beyond the understanding of how the conflict could have been avoided, respecting differences in people can help you better understand how to manage conflict in all aspects of your life.

OWN YOUR PEOPLE SKILLS...IN A FLASH

- You can be part of the problem, or part of the solution: the choice is yours.
- Raise your EQ by improving your self-awareness, self-regulation, motivation, empathy, and social skills. Treat people the way they want to be treated. Learn to respect and interact with as many personality styles as possible.
- Never respond when you're emotional or angry.
- Listen actively. Hear what is being said, and pay attention to what isn't being said.
- Don't judge. See somebody else's side of the story.
- Don't avoid conflicts. Rather, aspire to find the win-win collaboration that benefits both parties.
- Plan the most strategic time to engage in a conversation involving conflict resolution.
- Remember that the best way to defuse a conflict is to assume positive intent and refuse to go to war.

4 Own
YOUR VIRTUAL SPACE

Social media is called social media for a reason. It lends itself to sharing rather than horn-tooting.

– AUTHOR MARGARET ATWOOD

Now that you're more conscious of your interpersonal space, we're going to take your presence to a whole new level. Your personal brand is equally affected by your virtual presence. How you answer the phone, reply to emails, text, tweet, and present yourself in cyberspace all becomes a reflection of the overall perception you choose to create.

Whether you participate in it or not, social media is here to stay. The days of hiding in your cubicle and just getting on with your job are over. And while cyberspace can be daunting for those who didn't grow up with it, if you don't adapt, evolve and harness the power of this virtual space, a world of opportunities can pass you by.

While speaking and training on this topic, we often hear the response, "Social media is overwhelming. It's a waste of time." And of course, we're all aware of the devastating potential it has to damage an individual's career. We've all seen prominent politicians, celebrity figures and successful professionals sabotage their reputations over inappropriate emails or tweets. Media and law consultant Emma Sadleir emphasizes that today we are *all* spokespeople for the companies we're employed by, and that the watchword is caution. "Don't underestimate the power in that," she says. "Anything that is not in the best interest of the company is a big no-no. This includes complaining about the company in any way; saying something nasty about a colleague, client or customer; airing dirty laundry; leaking confidential information; or slamming a competitor of your company."

As soon as something exists in digital format, it is out of your control. Warren Buffett once said that it takes 20 years to build a reputation and five minutes to ruin it. Sadleir gives it five seconds on social media. She says we should all manage our online profiles as if our bosses were watching.

In addition, it is important to be aware that your digital opinions have the potential to lurk in cyberspace for ever. "If you're 16 and you're on social media, and you have all these opinions and you're being mean...that's all being documented," warns South African media personality Angela Mdoda. "Everything I did when I was sixteen exists only in my memory and in the memories of the people I was with. But now, your life is out there. And, at twenty-six, you're not who you were at sixteen. Social media education is like sex education – by the time they ask about it, it's actually too late."

Social media is an increasingly important way to enhance your professional space, and these days it's more likely that others will encounter you online before they do in person. You may be surprised to find that you probably have an online presence already, even if you haven't created one!

When did you last Google yourself? Individuals, businesses, and groups are living their lives online, so the chances are that you're being branded in cyberspace whether you are consciously involved in the process or not. In all our workshops, we suggest that our participants Google themselves every few months. You might be surprised at what comes up. It could range from listings in alumni organizations to being tagged in old photographs from a forgotten December holiday, your old nursery school, or that staff party you wish you could forget.

When it comes to cyberspace, you need to start controlling what your prospective employer, an HR professional or a colleague in your company will see.

That doesn't mean you suddenly need to immerse yourself in social media to the extent that it consumes hours of your time, or that you need to create a profile on every social media platform that comes along. You do, however, need to understand what they are, learn how to use them, and decide which ones will work best for your personal brand. Sadleir gives us some great advice when she says that we should use the platforms we feel most comfortable with.

MAKE THE MOST OF SOCIAL MEDIA

If navigated skillfully, the world of virtual interaction has a lot to offer. Despite its potential disadvantages, it's a wonderful platform to connect, find others and be found. There are plenty of smart opportunities that you can exploit to expand your presence, your network and your prospects. In the words of social networking expert and head of Trio Media Group, Denise Elsbree Smith, "You need to take this seriously, and you need to take the time to do it right."

Beatriz Rodriguez reminds us, "Don't underestimate your impact. Someone is always listening. The simplest activities are shaping your brand." This is as true with in-person encounters as well as social media interaction.

So, what *should* you be saying on social media?

We always say, if in doubt, leave it out. In other words, if you are not totally sure that what you are about to share is constructive, or congruent with the way you want to be seen, don't post it.

The key to maintaining our personal brands online is consistency: If you change who you are, what you like and how you feel every day, then people aren't going to know who you really are. The reason brands are successful is because people like what they know. If Coca-Cola tasted different every time you tasted it, you would just stop buying it. Personal branding is about authenticity, consistency and honesty – at all times.

Part of that consistency is your branding across all platforms. It's not going to help you if you have a professional presence on LinkedIn, but on Facebook you post party photos where you look like you've had one too many. People are viewing your brand across all platforms, so you need to be consistent. In the entertainment world, they say you're only as good as your last show. In social media, you're only as credible as your last post.

Whatever platforms you decide to focus on, there are three channels that we feel are key to boosting your virtual presence in the working world: LinkedIn, Twitter and Facebook.

LINKEDIN

Smith likens Facebook to a cocktail party. On the other hand, LinkedIn, the popular social network for business professionals, is more like an online business meeting. And with two new members joining every second, it's growing rapidly. A LinkedIn profile done right is more than just your online resume: it's a platform to celebrate your successes. On LinkedIn you can ensure that your achievements are recognized and that others know how to reach you with relevant opportunities.

If social media really isn't for you, we recommend that at the very minimum you have a complete LinkedIn profile that is as close to complete as possible, as LinkedIn maintains that users with complete profiles are 40 times more likely to receive opportunities. A completed profile includes the following:

- Your industry and location
- An up-to-date current position (with a description)
- Two past positions
- Your education
- Your skills (minimum of three)
- A profile photo
- At least 50 connections

If you're still not convinced, then consider this: in most industries, potential employers or new connections will probably find it strange if you're not on LinkedIn. These days, interviews and meetings start long before everyone actually meets in person. If someone wants to engage with you, the first place they'll check you out is on LinkedIn, and you need to make a good first impression.

The first thing they'll see when they click on your profile is your photograph, so use a professional image. Not a selfie. Not a party shot in your little black dress. This isn't a beauty contest; it's a professional platform. Do you look ready for that senior position? Your potential employer had better think so. "Be professional in all ways because LinkedIn is a professional, work-oriented site," says Troy Allen Johnson of Ambassador Social Media in Atlanta. "Casual pictures from your vacation or comic book versions of yourself for your profile picture are inappropriate unless you're seeking creative positions with Cartoon Network or Disney."

What viewers will see next is the line of text under your name. This is where you provide your title. Don't be shy: introduce yourself with a great headline – it should indicate what you do and what value you can bring. Your company's brand might be strong enough that it and your title are sufficient – like "Nadia Bilchik – Editorial Producer and Anchor, CNN." But you don't have to stick to traditional titles; you can get creative. For example, "Lynn Right – the blogger who thousands of people love to read every day."

Whatever you do, be authentic. Don't bring a thinly veiled sales pitch into your headline. Yes, you want to grab their attention and entice them to read further, but people see straight through sales pitches. Bring your personality into your profile. Picture yourself at a networking event or a client meeting. How would you introduce yourself? That's your authentic voice. Use it.

The rest of your profile should support your headline. Your summary comes next. It's the essence of who you are and what you do. In the same way that you need to think carefully about how you present yourself in person, so the same level of conscious thought has to go into how you present yourself online. The more meaningful your summary is, the more time your readers will give you. It helps to think of this summary as your 30-second elevator pitch. Picture yourself at that networking event again. After you've introduced yourself, how do you describe what you do, what your company does? Be accurate, succinct and compelling.

LinkedIn also gives you the opportunity to establish your credibility further in sections like experience, skills and endorsements, education, additional info, honors and awards, and recommendations. Make the most of these sections and remember to keep it relevant to your profile as a whole. Johnson says that the two absolutely essential items in a LinkedIn profile are completeness and professionalism. "Take advantage of all options within your profile, including a summary of all the relevant work/volunteer experience positions you've held with keywords and phrases relevant to your industry," Johnson says. "The digital real estate in your profile is precious – don't let it go to waste."

Once you've completed your profile like an all-star, get to know some of the LinkedIn tools that will help you build social capital with people in your network.

Join forums and groups. Not only can you add value by sharing knowledge, but posting thoughtful questions and useful answers can build your credibility and raise your visibility. In fact, the best questions and answers give people a reason to look at your profile.

You can also build connections and get endorsed on LinkedIn. You can get recommendations from those colleagues, clients and employers who speak convincingly about your abilities and your performance. Ask them to focus on a specific skill or a personality trait that drives their opinion of you. And make sure you endorse others too. Don't say the same thing about everyone; show that you've given it some thought, and that your sense of perception is on the mark. Johnson gives some valuable advice when he tells us to value the importance of recommendations over endorsements on LinkedIn.

So how can LinkedIn help with people you're meeting in person? If you are about to meet someone for the first time, look them up on LinkedIn ahead of time, establish a connection and tell them that you're looking forward to connecting.

Another way to use LinkedIn in the real world is to use it to set up a meeting. Imagine you're at a networking event and you spot someone you don't know yet but would love to meet. Maybe she has your dream job, or she runs a great company that you would like to work for one day. Would you ever walk up to this person and blurt out a question, or request her time, without context, gratitude, or even an introduction? Probably not. But it happens all the time on LinkedIn.

The amazing thing about LinkedIn is that it allows you to connect one-on-one with nearly anyone in the world. But so many people are wasting this opportunity by sending brief or automated messages. We see it happening all the time. People send messages that don't give the recipient any meaningful reason to connect. "Can you help me?" or "I'd like to connect with you on LinkedIn" are lazy, unprofessional messages that are highly unlikely to get a response.

You're much more likely to make the connections you're looking for when you spend a few more minutes crafting a personalized note.

WRITING A LINKEDIN INMAIL THAT'LL GET OPENED

If you want your message to be opened and taken seriously, use an effective InMail framework. Grab attention with a relevant and interesting subject line and consider opening with an acknowledgment of your recipient's success. You should then briefly talk about who you are, and why are you reaching out. Furnish your mail with one or two key insights and end with a strong call to action. Follow these tips:

- Write a strong subject line. Make the reason for your InMail clear and give the recipient a compelling reason to respond to you.
- Keep your mail short. Be brief, polite and to the point. You'll put them off with a long thesis.
- Start a conversation. Avoid talking *at* the person, or coming across like you're giving a sales pitch. Rather, work on developing a conversation with the person you want to engage.
- Find a common contact. People immediately assume it's going to be more spam when they receive an InMail, so start with a common connection, if possible, like "Carol from Company X suggested I contact you." This immediately makes your recipient more open to reading your InMail.
- Find a common interest. If you haven't been referred by anyone, find a common interest, or refer to something your recipient has achieved or created that can serve as a basis for connecting and help you establish some familiarity.
- Be mindful. Just because you have access to someone's attention, doesn't mean that this person is suddenly your friend. This is a tool to establish your virtual presence; don't abuse it. Give the people you interact with the respect they deserve.

LinkedIn is an incredible tool when you need a specific result. But even when you don't have a grand purpose, it's good to remain active on it. Remind your contacts that you're doing good work. Share relevant links with others in your industry, keep your profile current, and update your information whenever you have another accomplishment to share.

TWITTER

At this point, most of us have heard of celebrities or politicians who count their "Twitter Followers" by the million, and this powerful social networking tool seems to carry the keys to fame and career success. Even so, many participants in our workshops admit that they're quite intimidated by Twitter, or that they just don't get it.

While nobody is suggesting that you immediately start tweeting furiously at the crack of dawn, there is no question that there are huge benefits in getting to know this widely used social media platform. One way you can get your feet wet and start demystifying Twitter is to become a passive user.

As a passive user, you don't have to tweet anything at all. Simply set up an account and follow your company, industry peers and people who interest you. That way you can be the best spectator ever, and keep up with whatever is happening in your field. Give it a try – see what they're saying on Twitter. You'll soon find out why it's such a huge part of our culture and an important tool for news-gathering. You may even find it's precisely the connecting and branding opportunity you've been looking for.

Twitter is a bit like a megaphone for the content on all your other sites, and it works extremely well as a complementary site to leverage your own website, Facebook page or blog. It's also a community, but before you can expect others to take interest in you, you need to take an interest in them. With that community outlook in mind, you'll find that Twitter can be a valuable resource to take your virtual presence to another level.

According to consultant and online marketing author Mitch Meyerson, it all starts with a strategy. He suggests that in order to make your Twitter experience successful, you should begin by asking the following key questions:

- What are you trying to accomplish on Twitter?
- What's the value you bring to the conversation?
- What types of people do you want to connect with?
- How will you feature your products and services without being pushy?
- What's your plan for eventually moving people from Twitter to other places (like your email list, phone list, Facebook page or Skype) to deepen the relationship?

If that's all a bit much for you right now, you can start small by simply asking yourself, *What do I want my online presence to say about me?* Once you have decided on that, it all becomes much easier. Now all you have to do is say it in 140 characters or less.

The first step to getting started on Twitter is ensuring that your profile is set up correctly. Choose an easy-to-remember username (also known as a Twitter handle) like @EmmaSadleir and don't be tempted to hide behind an image that isn't you. People are often wary of those who seem to hide their identities. Your Twitter bio is where you get to tell people who you are in 160 characters. Be authentic and interesting. People almost always scan your bio before they decide whether to follow you, so think about the people you'd like to interact with on Twitter. What interests do you share? What can you learn from each other? What is it that draws you in about their bios? Remember that Twitter is a search engine too, so optimize your profile by including relevant keywords and links to your website in your bio.

Start following people you already know by looking for them in Twitter's search box. Following someone on Twitter is the same thing as adding someone on Facebook as a friend, except that they don't see your updates unless they choose to follow you too. Generally, the best way to get followers is to add people based on your mutual interests. Once you begin following others, you'll find that many of them will then follow you in return.

According to Mark Schaefer, author of *The Tao of Twitter*, developing solid connections is dependent on three factors: targeted connections, meaningful content and authentic helpfulness.

TARGETED CONNECTIONS

The starting point is to surround yourself with people you are interested in and, more importantly, who might be interested in you and what you have to say. In the world of Twitter, it is all about establishing meaningful connections. Like Shaefer says, "Connections lead to awareness. Awareness leads to trust. Trust is the ultimate catalyst to business as well as personal benefits."

MEANINGFUL CONTENT

Not sure what to tweet about? Start with what interests you – anything from business and industry news to a new restaurant you just went to. But only tweet if you have something valuable to say. Don't tell us what you ate for breakfast or how many calories you burned at the gym.

Another powerful way to generate content is to spend time reading tweets by other people and to retweet them if you think they will be of value to your own followers. Shaefer maintains that content is "the currency of the social web." The way we build connections is by sharing relevant content. Because tweets are limited to 140 characters, think carefully – not just about your content, but about your structure too. Make sure the first few words are powerful enough to catch attention.

Your Twitter content is not limited to just words. You can also share links and post photos and videos. You can start a discussion with someone or a company by using their @username in your tweet. Or you can make use of searchable hashtags by putting the # symbol before a keyword or phrase with no spaces #likethis. When you hashtag something like #Leadership, you're telling users that the content in your tweet is related to leadership. People searching the topic will be able to find your tweet, and you.

If you'd prefer to reach out to one of your followers privately, you can do so by sending a direct message. Simply tap the Messages icon and click "New Message," or select "Message" from the person's profile page.

AUTHENTIC HELP AND GENEROSITY

If LinkedIn is a business meeting, and Facebook is a cocktail party, then Twitter is your soapbox and your platform. But no one wants to listen to someone who only talks about themselves. Do you have something to say and to share that is of value to someone else? Show a genuine interest in others. If someone has helped you out, thank them publicly. Offer help to others without an agenda. Shaefer says that people fail on Twitter because they cannot fake authenticity and "people will figure you out pretty quickly if you are only out there for your own agenda."

FACEBOOK

Facebook is another excellent way to stay connected, particularly if your network is spread across the country and overseas. But it's not just for personal interaction; it's also a *working* cocktail party. And like Smith says, "It's supposed to be fun!"

Most people, however, feel that Facebook is the one area of their online communication where they are entitled to personal privacy. In fact, one of the most common rebuttals we hear is, "My personal life is personal and my professional life is professional – and I want them kept separate."

How you present yourself online is always a personal choice, and how available you make yourself, both personally and professionally, is typically driven by many personal factors. We have seen numerous perspectives on this, and none are wrong, but if you are trying to maximize your virtual presence and open yourself up to all the opportunities out there, the odds are more in your favor if you have productive, positive profiles in multiple places – Facebook included.

More and more businesses and organizations are using Facebook, and the more available you are, the more real, believable and approachable your profiles appear to be.

As Ranka Jovanovic, a pioneer in the online media space says, "You can't go without social media, but you also need to find a balance between your private life and your public activities. It is a tricky balancing act to do all that because there's a lot of privacy we've given up anyway just by participating. So be you. Focus on being the genuine person you are across all those boundaries."

If you decide to limit Facebook to your personal life, be aware that (privacy measures notwithstanding) it's still quite likely that your professional contacts like supervisors or even potential employers could come across your Facebook profile. The extent to which employers can use questionable and negative Facebook posts as grounds for demoting or terminating an employee is already becoming a hot legal issue.

Check your company's policies, procedures and guidelines regarding Facebook and other social media sites and be sure to follow them. People have lost jobs for posting things on Facebook they shouldn't have, particularly when they're working in fields like healthcare or education, where confidentiality is required by law.

And never vent on Facebook. If you are having a bad day at work, resist the urge to tell the world about it on your Facebook status, unless you are very sure that this is an opinion you want to share with friends and possibly many, many others. Depending on your privacy settings, if a friend shares what you say, your thoughts can travel around the world faster than a speeding bullet!

Be aware that others can tag you in photos or posts, and when you click the "like" button on other pages, groups and entities, remember that this will reflect who you are as a person. Think carefully about what you want to communicate about yourself to the outside world.

It is for all these reasons that you should review your security settings regularly. Facebook is known to make frequent privacy changes, so ensure you have selected your preferred settings. The security settings on your account will affect who can see your information, your posts and the posts of others on your timeline. You can make your profile and your timeline as public or private as you'd like, but be aware that many experts warn users that these security settings can be unreliable. As one HR professional pointed out, "If anybody has a camera, behave. You can control what you do, but you can't control what others put up."

If you prefer to keep personal and professional separate on Facebook, you can create a business page for your professional activities in addition to your personal profile.

Facebook is the world's largest social networking platform. If you approach your professional presence on Facebook with a little grace and polish, it can be a fun and interactive professional networking tool that can help you build stronger relationships and showcase your achievements.

•••

As a whole, social media is a tool that can make or break your virtual presence. When in doubt, Sadleir suggests the "billboard test." All you need to do is imagine a giant billboard with a picture of you. It includes your full name and the company you work for. It's there for all the world to see. Now imagine that what you're about to post will appear on that billboard too. Do you still want to say it?

Professionals who use social media to promote their personal and business brands first carefully consider what their presence will be. "Not everyone's personality is suited to be interacting on social media," says one of our highly successful colleagues. "Don't outsource it and don't ever be contrived," she added. "It is easy to damage your personal brand if you do not communicate consistently and in accordance with what is expected from you as a person in a specific profession. If you are a doctor and you want to be on social media, then you have to be mindful of your comments. You can't ever be too informal – posting selfies of yourself at parties drinking or smoking as an internist would simply not work for your public profile. You will be judged by social media, your peers and your patients. Many people have damaged themselves by making comments on or retweeting content that is inappropriate for the profession they represent. Twitter, in particular, takes no prisoners, and you have to choose your words carefully or *be damned*."

So, if you're using any social media platform for the first time, take it slowly and carefully. Be strategic and study people you relate to in terms of brand personalities. Watch how they act on Twitter or Instagram; get a sense of what the social community thinks about them; do the research; and understand what works and what doesn't on any platform before you just start having conversations or posting pictures or links. Social media can be brutal if you err, so always think before you tweet or post!

Whether you choose to network on just one social networking platform, all three of the platforms we've recommended, or if you feel you need to include others like Google+, Pinterest or Instagram, there are some general guidelines you should always be aware of no matter what sites you're active on.

MINDING YOUR SOCIAL MEDIA MANNERS

- Be authentic. Be honest and let people see your personality.
- Be respectful. Freedom of speech comes with the responsibility to respect other points of view.
- Mind your language. Be polite. Don't use expletives, inappropriate language or too many abbreviations. And check your spelling.
- Don't shout. Posting in uppercase is like shouting in the real world.
- Always remember: when in doubt, leave it out.

And to truly make the most of social media, use every opportunity to extend the conversation and the relationship by taking it offline. Connect in a deeper way through email, a phone call, or even better, with a face-to-face meeting.

UNDERSTAND EMAIL ETIQUETTE

Although texting is quickly taking over, email is probably still the most common way we communicate virtually. Unfortunately, it is remarkably easy to annoy people, destroy friendships and derail your career with a thoughtless piece of electronic communication.

Most of us have been using personal emails for so long that we sometimes forget to apply a separate and much stricter set of rules to business emails. Email is much more than just a means to communicate; it also forms part of the reputation you're working so hard to establish. In essence, every email you send is a reflection of yourself.

Emails are instant. With that in mind, start by becoming more aware of your intention, your tone and your content before you hit that send button. When you finish typing up an email, try to trigger your mental "pause" button and run your eyes over your content with absolute focus before you send it off.

Never email in anger; rather hit that mental pause button. Once you've had time to cool down, you can email with purpose, not frustration. Always keep in mind that between a request and a response there lies a pause – you don't have to answer immediately. If you wouldn't say it face-to-face, it has no place in an email. If you aren't sure, ask a friend with an objective opinion to read the email before you send it. We've seen so many people, from entry-level assistants to high-powered executives, make themselves look petty and powerless by getting caught up in defensive and "CYA" (cover your ass) email wars. Don't do it! If your emotions are running high, save your email as a draft and come back to it once you're feeling more settled.

Take a moment to check your tone, even if you're not feeling particularly emotional. Emails take on the attitude that the *recipient* assumes the sender has – and that can very often be far less positive than the sender intends. Re-read your message through that lens. If you have to, rewrite that email so that no one, not even someone who thinks you're angry, could get the wrong message.

Being mindful is probably the most important tool for a successful email. When you are present, you are aware of what you are writing, and you are aware of how it comes across.

If you're not in a hurry, you can also avoid making mistakes like forgetting to double-check any awkward changes your autocorrect has decided to make. In fact, if you're in the habit of typing and sending messages from your phone, it's a good idea to turn autocorrect off completely. You'll be surprised what your "smart" phone thinks you are trying to type.

In all your business email communications, remember to keep it professional. Don't forward jokes, chain mails or spam – especially when there are attachments. These attachments may contain viruses and there's probably no worse way to sabotage a business relationship than to accidentally send someone a virus that takes over their computer.

Beware of getting too comfortable with text-speak, especially with your colleagues. If you are the type of person who feels friendly and relaxed with almost anyone, you may be quite comfortable signing off emails with "c u soon," or replying to an email with "lol." But apart from making you look less professional, it can also muddy the waters and lead to misunderstandings. When you wrote "lol," did you mean "laugh out loud" or "lots of love"?

Save your text-speak and abbreviations for friends and family. Use words in their full form, with the correct spelling, when you're writing to new acquaintances, colleagues, customers and bosses. Polished writing skills are as reflective of your overall presence as the way you speak or present yourself in person. Craft your virtual communications with the same care as you would give to an important document.

It's also really smart to be mindful of what annoys other people when it comes to email communication in general. In all our groups across the country and around the world, we find many similar pet peeves. Apart from misspellings, text-speak and emoticons (always at the top of the list), people do not like receiving quick replies that show a lack of understanding, emails that ramble on forever, or emails that don't include any direct information or that don't answer the question at all. Use the CC and "reply all" functions with caution. Nobody appreciates it when emails include CCs that are clearly intended to be intimidating or when they get a round of "reply all" emails that are not relevant to them.

SET UP YOUR EMAIL

Whether your objective is a simple request, a pitch for new business or purely something informative, you want your email to make an impact on the person reading it. Here are some guidelines to help you compose the most effective email:

Create an email signature that includes your name, your contact information and links to your relevant social media sites. Remember to keep your email signature simple though, otherwise it will clog up your email and may even get caught in spam filters.

It's also important to give proper thought to the out-of-office response you leave on your email account. Do you follow grammatical rules? Do you leave a substitute set of contact details for someone in your team to assist in your absence? Apart from the obvious – stating you are out of the office – have you ever considered how you can use your out-of-office replies to boost your virtual presence? For example, if you are traveling on business, you could briefly share where you are going, and what you hope to accomplish. You can assure your correspondent that you will respond to them in a timely fashion.

MAKE SURE IT'S THE RIGHT PERSON!

Have you ever sent a confidential email to the wrong person? Take your time when you're inserting the email address. Make sure it's the *right* Jane. Make sure you've spelled the email address correctly and you've got allthe dots in all the right places. And when it comes to the body of your email, make sure you spell their name correctly there too! It is insulting to misspell someone's name, so pay attention to the details, and get it right.

COME UP WITH A SHORT AND CONCISE SUBJECT LINE

Keep your subject line short but descriptive. It may seem trivial to you, but the subject line of your email can be the difference between your email being opened or overlooked. An appropriate subject line will give a clear indication of the content of the email. Make it as compelling, but as brief and informative as possible. If you're picking up an old email to locate an address, change the subject line to be relevant to the new conversation. Don't just hit reply with the old subject line if it has nothing to do with today's content – you'll just confuse the situation and come off looking lazy and unprofessional.

START AT THE BEGINNING

Introduce yourself. If the person you're emailing is a new contact or even an existing contact who may not know what you do or what company you're from, take the time to introduce yourself properly. It may sound incredibly obvious to you, but it's astounding how often basic introductions are overlooked. We sometimes see people launching into an entire sales pitch without setting the context of where they are from and why they are sending the email.

THINK ABOUT HOW YOU'RE GOING TO SAY IT

Be clear about the purpose of your communication and about who your audience is.

BE SUCCINCT

Keep your emails short and concise, especially when you're emailing people in senior roles. When busy people see verbose emails, they often ignore them without even thinking twice – or worse, delete them.

USE PARAGRAPHS

When you limit each paragraph to one main idea and its supporting details, it helps you organize your thoughts and clarify your message. In addition, visually breaking up the text makes the email easier to read.

BE AWARE OF YOUR TONE

Tone will affect the response you receive. Be polite and work those good manners: *Please, thank you, I would appreciate...*They all go a long way towards making the recipient more open to your request and help set a fitting tone.

Not everyone you email is your friend, so maintain an appropriate level of formality depending on whom you are communicating with. If it's a new contact, "Dear..." or even "Good morning" or "Good afternoon" is probably more suitable than an informal "Hi there." And don't forget to include titles like Dr. if applicable. Keep your writing clear, avoid slang and don't be too colloquial or chatty.

Exclamation marks, writing in caps and using emoticons all affect the way your email will be interpreted. Capital letters and exclamation marks give the impression that you're angry and yelling. And while emoticons might be perfectly acceptable when you're sending an email to a friend, they can have a negative impact in the formal corporate space, sabotaging the overall way you are perceived.

When you're not sure about how your email will be interpreted, no matter how much you try to finesse it, pick up the phone instead or set up a meeting where you can reassure the person with positive body language and a warm and genuine smile – because once that email has left your outbox, there's no way of getting it back.

SIGN OFF GRACIOUSLY

Don't leave the email open-ended without a formal closing. "Best regards" is suitable for formal interactions, as well as for people who are colleagues. Once you have developed a rapport with someone, you can change it to something more approachable, such as "Warm regards," which is slightly less formal while still maintaining a sense of respect for the other person.

DON'T FORGET SPELLCHECK

Use spellcheck and check your grammar. Always. In the same way that showing up in scruffy clothes gives the impression you don't care, so does sending off a badly put together email. Spelling errors and incorrect grammar reflect poorly on you and undermine your intelligence. Writing coach Leslie Ayres says that even if you weren't hired to write for a living, writing well (whether in emails, PowerPoint presentations or memos) is an important element of every job.

Here are some common grammatical and spelling errors to avoid:

- **Confusing possessive pronouns with contractions:** *You're* means *you are*. *Who's* is short for *who is*, and *it's* is short for *it is*. Even though we use an apostrophe to denote possession in the case of nouns, like the dog's bone, we do not use an apostrophe when using possessive pronouns. That coat is *yours*; the dog hurt *its* paw; and it is not clear *whose* cellphone went off in the middle of a meeting.
- **There is no such word as "alot":** Lori likes to drink *a lot* of coffee, and our children expect us to *allot* (dole out) favors fairly.
- **Every day vs everyday:** Every day is usually two words, and only becomes one word when used as an adjective to describe a noun. We go to work *every day*, and getting caught in traffic is an *everyday* experience in big cities like Atlanta.
- **Sentence fragments:** Our conversations are full of sentence fragments. "Because I said so!" is something your parents might have said, but don't start a sentence with words like because, since, when, whenever, while, and as, without completing the thought, as in *Since the weather has changed, I have started wearing closed shoes to work.*
- **Run-on sentences and comma splices:** These happen when you try use a comma to join together clauses that could be sentences on their own. *Writing well is an important skill, it helps enhance your professional presence* is incorrect. You can edit that sentence as follows: *Writing well is an important skill; it*

helps enhance your professional presence. Or: *Writing well is an important skill because it helps enhance your professional presence.* Finite clauses (that is, phrases that include both a subject and a verb) can be linked with a semi-colon or conjunction – or you can even separate them into two sentences, using a period at the end of the first clause.

- **Subject-verb agreement:** A singular subject must have a singular verb, and a plural subject must agree with a plural verb. The staff members *are* meeting, but the staff *is* meeting.

Most word-processing programs have spellcheck with the capacity to highlight errors and suggest changes, but these systems are not infallible. It never hurts to be aware of common errors like the ones we've just mentioned. There are also numerous websites that can give you grammar and composition pointers to help you enhance your vocabulary.

KNOW WHEN TO PRESS SEND

While your auto-response takes care of itself, your emails aren't going to send themselves. When do you send that concise, clear and professional email you've just written? So many of us end up logging on after hours or over the weekend just to get some quiet time without any distractions. Is it acceptable to email someone at 10 pm just because that's when it suits you? There's a fine line between looking diligent and dedicated and becoming downright intrusive. We need to be aware of the timings of our emails – and that timing all depends on who you happen to be emailing.

If your boss or colleague requested that information from you, then by all means send it through. However, if you are emailing a new contact, or a senior person in your company, hold off until the next morning. If you do have to email them at night, make it clear that you know it's a late hour and that you do not expect a response from them until business hours. If, for example, you're catching up on some work over the weekend, let the person you're emailing know that you don't expect a response before Monday. That way they won't perceive you as being invasive.

Whether you're sending your emails within or outside of business hours, if you don't receive a response in due course, don't be afraid to follow up. Often, opportunities are missed or misunderstandings happen because "they didn't reply to my email." Don't sit there wondering whether or not the email was received or if the content of the email was understood. When there's silence, follow up with a call. A personal phone call or a one-on-one meeting will always win.

YOUR SMARTPHONE: FRIEND AND FOE

Being in constant communication has become the norm. Laptops, tablets and, of course, super smartphones are the slim, shiny devices that make it all happen. More than anything else, smartphones have given us the freedom of mobility – and an office in our back pockets. We can send and receive emails, keep current with the latest news, book flights while listening to our favorite songs, schedule meetings, take conference calls, update our social networks, and even do a little mobile banking. All without being tied to our desks.

But as useful as they can be, the bewitching quality of our smartphones can blind us to their impact on our overall persona. Seemingly trivial details, like our choice of ringtone, our addiction to texting, and the smartphone's enormous capacity for entertainment and distraction, can detract from our overall presence, whether we're aware of it or not.

Remember that we're all building the perception of our personal brands moment by moment through every small interaction, both verbal and non-verbal. And that includes what we do with our smartphones. We cannot choose which interactions people will remember, but we can choose how we behave during those interactions. A lot is being said these days about how much people lose themselves in their smartphones at the expense of what's going on in the real world around them, and for good reason. Have you ever sat at a dinner table and noticed that everyone's glued to their phones instead of engaging with the people right in front of them? It may be acceptable in some social circles, but it's not good for business.

While smartphone use is appropriate in some professional environments, such as tweeting during a conference using the event's official hashtag, there are other instances in the work environment when constantly referring to your phone, replying to messages, updating your status on Facebook, and taking selfies is not going to do your professional reputation any good. If you're self-aware, you will know when you are in a place where it isn't appropriate to text or to answer a call, especially when you're in a more formal environment.

There are many communication channels for us to use, and many of us don't always stop to think which channel (or which time or setting) would be the most appropriate. In one of our workshops, a senior executive shared her very annoyed response to an inappropriate use of WhatsApp. She gave an example of a time when someone in her team sent a WhatsApp message, complete with atrocious spelling and grammar, to excuse herself from coming into the office because she was sick. Both the team leaders and the executive felt they deserved a phone call and an explanation of the situation, not the cavalier WhatsApp they received instead. It was viewed as disrespectful and greatly affected their perception of the unwitting WhatsApp sender.

When you're wondering which would be better, whether to phone or to send a text, be aware of the situation and be aware of whom you are talking to. Put yourself in their shoes, and try to see it from their perspective. How would they want to hear this information or news that you are about to share? It may not be your way, but how you choose to communicate will affect their overall opinion of you.

As workshop and corporate event facilitators, we're acutely aware of generation gaps, especially in the corporate world. It's a gap that gives rise to constant debates about virtual etiquette and communication in the workplace because everybody has specific views on how they should communicate. For example, Baby Boomers (born between 1946 and 1964) prefer phone calls and face-to-face meetings to texting and teleconferencing. Millennials (born between the early 1980s to the early 2000s) grew up with mobile technology, and are far more flexible and comfortable with communicating on mobile devices, social media platforms and apps.

In order to prevent technology wars, sit down and have a conversation with your boss, colleagues, employees and even your clients, and find a way to communicate that works best for all of you. Millennials might, for example, be viewed as being disengaged or rude for using their smartphones in meetings when they're actually taking notes or even sourcing relevant information that could push the entire meeting forward. Make it your business to know how people want to be communicated with. Don't make assumptions. Just because it works for you doesn't mean it works for everybody else.

TEXTING AND WHATSAPPING: THE RULES OF ENGAGEMENT

Texting and WhatsApping are often the most immediate and reliable ways of getting a response, especially with Millennials, but they're not always the right way to go. Texts and WhatsApp messages are particularly useful when you need to give your boss the heads-up that an urgent email is incoming or to make one of your team members aware that a tight deadline is about to land on their desk. But, when you've been ordered home by your doctor for a week, pick up the phone, dial the number and talk to your boss or HR department. If you're too sick to call, a formal email is better than a casual text message.

When you do choose to send a text to someone in your business circle, keep it professional. Just like your email communications, skip the acronyms, the slang and the emoticons. Take the time to use the right words in their full form. Be brief and concise, but keep it clean. Do yourself a favor and do away with autocorrect, but use spellcheck whenever you can.

When your phone dings and it's a message for you, acknowledge receipt as soon as it's appropriate to do so. People don't like being ignored or feeling as if they've been left hanging for a response. Even if you don't have the time to reply with a lengthy answer or a thoughtful response right at that moment, send a quick note saying, "Thanks, will reply soon," or, "I'm in a meeting. I'll call you shortly." This ensures that you look responsive, but still gives you the time you need to respond properly.

Pay attention to every little detail of your personal brand because everything you communicate has an impact on your virtual presence, and that includes your WhatsApp profile picture. You don't think it's particularly meaningful? It is. Given that anyone with your cellphone number in their contacts has access to you on WhatsApp, it's important to ensure the profile image you use is a photo of you that creates a positive impression.

PHONE CALLS, MESSAGES AND VOICEMAIL

The good, old-fashioned phone call. With today's rapidly advancing technologies and the myriad of communication platforms, the phone conversation is becoming increasingly underrated. But after a manic exchange of urgent emails and frenzied text messages, sometimes there's nothing better than a personal phone call.

When you do decide to call someone, however, check with them that it's a convenient time to chat. If you happen to catch someone in the middle of a task or a meeting, they'll probably try to end the call as soon as possible, and that can be extremely frustrating for both parties. Remember to identify yourself (don't say just say, 'Hi, it's me,' and assume they'll automatically recognize your voice), and ensure you have an end goal in mind before you make the call. It will make you come across as more focused.

If you get their voicemail, don't allow yourself to be caught off-guard, leaving a rambling message about why you phoned. Plan ahead. Give a succinct reason for your phone call and a clear call to action with your return number.

Speaking of voicemails, how's yours? On a scale from one to ten, how would you rate your voicemail message? Forget about hiding behind standardized voicemail messages ("You have reached the number ..."). It doesn't make you seem more mysterious or powerful. It makes you seem apathetic. In a world where things are becoming more and more remote and impersonal, people are yearning for that personal connection. Give it to them. Create a personal voicemail that projects enthusiasm, energy and professionalism. Since there are so many people who automatically shy away from leaving messages on voicemail, your voicemail should affirm that the caller has reached the right person and make them comfortable enough to leave a message.

Even your voicemail can have a powerful effect on your overall presence, so remember to put some thought into how you deliver it. Everything you do and say contributes to the overall impression you create.

Work with lines like, "Thanks so much for calling. I am not available at the moment, so please leave your name and number. I look forward to getting back to you as soon as possible." Or try, "I am in meetings all day, so feel free to text me or email me on ..."

If you decide to take the call instead of letting it go to voicemail, don't sound bored, distracted, irritated, or anxious. If you answer with a negative mindset, the caller will probably misinterpret your tone as reflecting how you feel about them. Even if your anger does happen to be directed at the person on the other end of the line, remember that it's never a good idea to respond when you're in a negative emotional state. And as for those ringtones? Feel free to claim your individuality with your favorite tune, but when you find yourself in a professional setting, play it safe and keep your phone on silent (or vibrate). There's a time and a place for everything, and that Annual General Meeting might not be the time to proclaim your undying love for the latest hit song.

That slim little handheld device may be your personal link to the world, but it can also destroy those precious links if it is used without being mindful. So, take care to treat everything with your name on it as a reflection of you.

OWN YOUR VIRTUAL SPACE...IN A FLASH

- Be consistent and authentic across all social platforms.
- Be as respectful and polite as you would be in person.
- Google yourself every few months. You are in control of what others see.
- Check your company's policies and guidelines regarding social media.
- Start with LinkedIn if you're exploring how social media can benefit you professionally.
- Never answer a call, send an email or post a comment on social media when you're in a state of heightened emotion.
- Press your mental pause button before you send an email or post a status: reflect, rethink, retype, and then send.
- Be succinct. Keep your emails short and concise.
- When typing an email, remember to introduce yourself and sign the email off in a professional way.
- Save your text-speak and abbreviations for friends and family.
- Be clear about the purpose of your communication, and understand your audience.
- Stop to think about which medium of communication would be the most appropriate for the situation.
- Bring the online conversation into the real world with a phone call or a meeting.

5 Own
YOUR TIME

The key is in not spending time, but in investing it.

– STEPHEN R. COVEY

We want to be everything. Actually, it's more than that. We want to be the *perfect* everything.

We want to be at the top of our game, and at the same time we want to be the world's best mother, daughter, sister, wife and friend. And we want to look *good* doing it all.

Open any women's magazine and the rhetoric says it all in article after article, reinforcing the belief that it is possible to be everything to everyone. We're told we can do it all. We just have to download nice little work-life balance pie charts and divide our life's areas into neat little segments and everything will be just fine.

Except, it doesn't work out that way. Life inevitably gets in the way and we find that we don't really have the time or the energy to be the perfect everything. Then, we feel guilty because somehow we're not quite managing to embody our own image of *superwoman*. We wonder what we're doing wrong, what magic secrets we don't know about and how everybody else makes it all seem so easy. But we don't give up. There must be a way. So, we push harder. And it all becomes even more challenging because we're always reachable, because work becomes more and more demanding, and we push ourselves more than ever.

When we realize all over again that there's never enough time or energy to do it all, we lather on great big dollops of guilt; we lose our confidence and we lose ourselves. We're so caught up in our crazed efforts to be everything to everyone that we forget about putting ourselves into the equation at all. And instead of taking a little time out for ourselves when we're exhausted, or low on confidence or losing direction, we keep striving to make it all perfect.

Does any part of this sound familiar?

According to a 2013 survey by LinkedIn, our definition of success has changed. Ten years ago, 56% of modern women valued having a high salary while 39% wanted to find balance between work and life. Today, the scales have changed: Women's sense of success is now defined by finding balance between work and life (63%) versus 45% who value a high salary.

Most women would rather see a greater balance in their lives than in their bank accounts. Where exactly is this frustratingly elusive work-life balance? It always seems to be dangling just out of reach. There's a simple reason. And it's really simple.

It doesn't exist.

There's no such thing as work-life balance.

The perfect balance is a complete myth, so forget about trying to do it all. That pursuit of perfection? Stop the proverbial treadmill. It's time to disembark. You don't have to feel guilty and stressed all the time. Just focus on doing the best you can with the time you have. You can heighten your productivity, lower your anxiety, invest in yourself a little more, and bridge the gap between work and your personal life...but you have to let go of perfectionism first.

THE WORK-LIFE BALANCE MYTH

We spoke about the relentless pursuit of perfection in Chapter 1, and we're going to talk about it again – because you cannot truly own your headspace or your confidence until you let go of the concept of the ideal you. You cannot truly own your time and your energy until you let perfectionism go. As women, our pursuit of 100% is so deeply ingrained that it just keeps sneaking up on us; we're not even aware that we keep striving for precision in all our many roles.

Instead, we tell ourselves we're just not quite good enough. So, going forward from this moment on, it would be wise to take the advice of Brené Brown and have the courage to be imperfect. Brown says that the root of the word courage is *cor* – the Latin word for heart – and that the original definition of displaying courage was telling the story of who you are with your whole heart. Brown's own research revealed that the happiest, most fulfilled people are the ones who have had the courage to be imperfect, to embrace vulnerability and to be authentic. They are the ones who were willing to let go of who they thought they *should* be and who have embraced who they truly are.

Too often, we get caught up in these ideas of who we think we "should" be. Albert Ellis, the founder of the rational therapy movement, now known as Rational Emotive Behavior Therapy (REBT), refers to these ideal images of ourselves and our lives as "irrational beliefs." He goes on to say that an idea is irrational if it distorts reality, is illogical, prevents you from reaching your goals, and leads to unhealthy emotions. Discovering your irrational beliefs is the first step to overcoming them, but then you must carry out the second most important act of disputing them.

Ellis believes that the idea of self-esteem is "highly subjective and far too dependent on factors outside our control." It is, he adds, the cause of the "greatest emotional suffering in the twentieth century...We may rate our actions as good, bad, successful or unsuccessful, but this does not mean that it has to reflect our self-worth."

Doesn't this make you feel a great deal better already? Hopefully you are letting out a sigh of relief as you read this.

Letting go of the idea of being 100% at all times is fundamental to achieving so-called "balance." Beatriz Rodriguez, Director and Chief Diversity Officer at The Home Depot, says something has to give. "We much understand [our goal is] to achieve balance, not perfection." The way to achieve balance, though, means that sometimes pressing concerns require more focus at a particular time. Rodriguez says, "It is okay, if to accomplish an important last minute work requirement, I could not pull an A on a school test or my kid had to eat pizza." What we can't do, she says, is lose sight of the big picture, how everything is working together. "Someone once used sound as an analogy: a high pitch by itself would sound terrible, but when you have mixed levels of sound, some higher and some lower, that is when you achieve music."

The idea of perfectionism is about pleasing others and comparing ourselves to others. As women we often do this. We often compare ourselves to people we believe are more successful than we are: other women who seem richer, more together, thinner, and more productive. But other people's lives aren't always what they appear to be. You never really know the full truth of someone else's reality.

When you let go of perfection, you'll realize there is no such thing as the perfect balance either. We all have days when the scales of equilibrium tip in one direction or another, when you feel you have neglected something – either your home or family life isn't getting the time it deserves, or you haven't put enough energy into work. If you didn't have a great mom day but had a great work day, then that's okay. The next day might be different.

Author and professor at Harvard Business School, Rosabeth Moss Kanter, says, "You *can* have it all. It just won't all be perfect." Don't torture yourself over perfection. Exchange the word "perfect" for "good enough." By its very definition, "good" is a high standard. It may not be utterly faultless, but then again, what is? "Good" is wholesome, valuable, safe. "Good" is desirable.

On those days when you catch yourself striving for perfection all over again, berating yourself because you're not doing enough, don't have enough, that things should be better...STOP. Take yourself off autopilot, take a step back, and practice gratitude. Leading gratitude researcher, Robert Emmons, has defined gratitude as "a felt sense of wonder, thankfulness, and appreciation for life." We can *cultivate* gratitude by *practicing* gratitude. In fact, the benefits of developing an attitude of gratitude are well-researched and numerous. Emmons has found that people who practice gratitude through activities such as keeping a gratitude journal are more loving, forgiving and optimistic about the future. They exercise more frequently, report fewer illnesses and generally feel better about their lives. They are also less negative, simply because feelings like anger, bitterness and resentment are incompatible with their positive attitude.

Balance is very much like happiness – it is a mindset, and it's achieved by the daily choices we make. It is not a fixed concept, and there is no one-size-fits-all. Everyone achieves their own version of balance based on their own unique set of priorities and goals. For example, what work-life balance means to a single young person compared to what it means to a parent with two young children can be very different. We all have our own ways of doing things, and we all create our own combination of balance that works best for us. For working women with kids, it is difficult to work in the early evenings because it means missing out on special family time. For some people, balance means leaving the office early to be home by 6 pm, but then logging on again once the family commitments are covered. If this works for you, then great. Many companies are comfortable with flexible working arrangements as long as you deliver what is expected of you. Part of achieving balance is the ability to have these kinds of important conversations with your boss – we will give you more details on how to do this in Chapter 8.

Another critically important aspect of grasping the concept of balance is to understand the difference between being busy and being productive. Being busy does not necessarily yield the desired results. Being productive means you achieve your objectives in a set time frame. The length of time dedicated to a task does not define it as being productive or not. You can spend an entire day writing a proposal but not come close to completion; however, you can spend a focused two hours and get it done.

Have you ever been under pressure to meet a deadline and been concerned you wouldn't be able to get it done? And yet somehow you managed to pull it off? This is a clear example of Parkinson's Law which states that "work expands to fill the time available for its completion." Joel Falconer, editor and journalist, explains this concept. "This means that if you give yourself a week to complete a two-hour task, then (psychologically speaking) the task will increase in complexity and become more daunting so as to fill that week. It may not even fill the extra time with more work, but just stress and tension about having to get it done. By assigning the right amount of time to a task, we gain back more time and the task will reduce in complexity to its natural state."

Judy Dlamini, a medical doctor by training who then moved into investment banking and finally into entrepreneurship says her priority is family. "It doesn't mean I work any less," she says. "It simply means when it's my daughter's birthday or when I have to do something for my child, or support my husband in any way, then everything else becomes secondary." Dlamini frequently cites a story told by international author Robin Sharma about glass balls and rubber balls in a juggling act. "You'll drop balls – that's guaranteed. Just don't drop the glass balls. Rubber balls can bounce back. Certain relationships are your glass balls, and for me, it's my relationship with my husband and my kids."

Many of our interviewees who seem to have found a way of navigating the complex part of work-life balance don't see it as being a balance between two completely separate halves of their lives. They see it as an integration – a work-life integration, where everything works together as a larger part of the whole. They control the things they can, like their thoughts, their attitudes and their choices, and they let go of the things they can't control.

Arlette Guthrie coordinates a demanding job as Vice President for non-store Human Resources at The Home Depot with the needs of two school-age children by combining her home and work schedules into one calendar. She makes sure to provide her assistant with both her work schedule and the annual school calendar so that important events on both fronts are built in. "If I am in talent planning season and we are in round-the-clock succession meetings, then those aren't going to be the weeks that I'm going to chaperone for the field trip, but when the opportunity arises, I'm going to take those trips because I know that they are precious. I am not settled at work if I'm concerned about being absent from the children's lives. And I'm not settled at home if I'm concerned about being absent from work. So blending the two has just been important for me," she says.

"Creating more balance in your life has to do with making conscious choices and clearing out the physical, technical and emotional clutter that gets in the way of what really matters," says author Tricia Molloy. She recommends making a list of your typical responsibilities and going through a process of elimination to identify and delegate or drop those responsibilities that are not essential to your work and home life. She says, "You'll find that your energy and clarity will increase once you release those unnecessary obligations that have been bringing you down."

Never underestimate the power we have to control our thoughts. We may inadvertently be sabotaging ourselves with our judgmental inner dialogue and by constantly reprimanding ourselves. One of the ways to keep this in check is to practice what we learned in Chapter 1. Remember those Mind Sneakers? We need to replace words that create anxiety – like *I must, I should have, I have to* –

with more empowering words like *I can, I want to, I deserve*. Just by changing these thoughts, we start to trigger healthier attitudes within ourselves. And when it comes to controlling our choices, we have to learn to say "no."

For such a tiny word, it's remarkably difficult for so many of us to say. As women, we so often have a natural instinct to be liked and we so often fear that saying no will make us less likeable, that it will make us appear selfish. As a gender, we've been socialized to go out of our way to accommodate others. Turning down a request or an invitation can be extremely difficult, and when we do say no, we're often left with feelings of guilt. But the reality is that we need to maintain healthy boundaries. We cannot possibly accept every request or invitation that comes our way because we'll only end up over-extending ourselves. Saying no is a choice, and we need to learn how to make it a guiltless part of our vocabulary.

THE YES SANDWICH

Your time and energy are no less important than that of your co-workers, friends or acquaintances, so there is no reason to feel guilty about saying no. That said, it can still feel quite uncomfortable to deny a request. There are many different ways to say no and some are more bearable than others. We have a technique we like to call the "Yes Sandwich." It's an approach that allows you to turn down a request in a way that softens the blow and helps the other person not to take your "no" so personally.

- **Layer 1:** Begin by positively acknowledging the other person's intent. If they're asking for your help, it's because they feel you have worthwhile experience and insights to offer. If they're inviting you to an event, it's because they value your company. You can begin by saying something along the lines of, "Thank you so much for thinking of me," or, "I'm flattered that you've asked."
- **Layer 2:** This is where you graciously say no. Rather than simply turning down the other person, you can add a few words explaining why you're unable to give them what they're asking for, while letting them know they can still feel comfortable coming to you with future requests. Here's an example: "I'd like to give you a hand with this project. Unfortunately, though, my plate is pretty full right now and I don't think I'd do your project any justice. But feel free to reach out to me at another time if you'd like assistance with something similar."

- **Layer 3:** Offer an alternative. If you can't give them what they're asking for, there might be something else you can offer that demands less from you. If you're unable to help them with their project today, maybe you can schedule a time to sit down with them later in the week. Or perhaps you can refer them to someone else. Suggesting another option demonstrates that, while your priority is to uphold your own boundaries, you are also sensitive to their needs and you're willing to do what you can to support them.

Nadia was once faced with a situation where a colleague asked her to address a group of women at his company and offered a ride on his boat as a thank you. As a professional speaker, Nadia has a standard fee for addressing corporate companies. Accepting a boat ride in lieu of adequate payment would have meant chastising herself, resenting her colleague and feeling completely belittled. Then again, an absolute "No – I don't work for free. How can you expect me to talk for nothing?" would have offended her colleague and she would most likely never do business with that person or company again.

She thought about it and decided to respond via email using the Yes Sandwich technique: "I started with layer 1, thanking him graciously for inviting me to speak to his staff. In layer 2, I outlined a negotiated rate that I would be happy to offer his company instead. While there was no need for the third layer in this case, I did include various available date options, and left it open to him as to how he would like to proceed.

"The way I responded allowed me to keep my integrity. Always remember to pause before you respond to a request or an invitation – there are many ways to say no while still maintaining your own integrity and reputation."

Linda Kaplan Thaler, author of the best-selling book *The Power of Nice*, says that "no" shuts down possibilities, while "yes" opens them up. "Yessing your way to the top does not mean doing everyone else's bidding," she writes. "It simply means finding something to say yes to." For example, if your boss asks you to come in to work over the weekend after you have just worked three consecutive weekends in a row, instead of just saying no, you could respond by expressing your appreciation for being considered such an important part of the project, and then offer an alternative time when you can get the job done. That way, everybody wins.

The Yes Sandwich comes in many forms. The key is to learn to apply it to your specific situation.

OWN YOUR TODO LIST

There's a better way to do things than arriving at your desk in the morning and diving headfirst into the growing pile of things you have to do: the endless emails you have to reply to, calls you have to answer, meetings you have to attend, and groceries you have to grab when you finally head home that evening.

SCHEDULE IT

Everything.

That's what Michelle Livingstone does: "If I want to make sure that I do some networking, or that I exercise, or that I prepare for a meeting, everything goes on the calendar," she says. "I have one calendar for home and work, and everything that is important to me goes on it."

The golden rule of work-life integration is this: If you want it done, it must be scheduled. Schedule anything you want from working projects to personal tasks. Let's say you've been trying to get back into the gym for a while now, but it's just not happening because you keep telling yourself you'll fit it in "somewhere" and somehow every day something else ends up taking top priority. Or that tea with a friend you've been trying to do but haven't because everything else seems to swallow up your time to such an extent that you can't even find 20 minutes for a little solitude.

Schedule it in.

When you allocate a dedicated time slot to your gym session or tea with your friend in your diary, like you would a meeting, these things automatically become as important as that meeting. You're committed. It's the same with "me" time and getting your family life in check. You need to block out time on your calendar for you and your family as much as you need to for your business associates. Block out dinner on your calendar. Block out date nights. Keep Sundays as a sacred time with your family and friends. Put all these things on your calendar in advance each month and then treat them with the importance of any other meeting. If it gets scheduled, it gets done.

Arriving at the office with a clear list of priorities can mean the difference between haphazardly running to the supermarket every day to pick up dinner and doing the weekly (or monthly) shop all at once. Or, even better, automate the whole process by using an online service that delivers groceries. It may be a little more expensive, but it saves you from those impulse buys, and it will give you more free time than you can imagine!

Entrepreneur Tracey Webster takes a highly systematic approach to successful planning: "When it comes to planning your week, break up clearly the six priority goals you need to achieve in a week and the four actions you can do daily to get there," she says. "I used to write reams of to do lists and feel overwhelmed when I had twenty things to do the next day. I went for coaching about it, and my coach advised me to prioritize what is urgent and what can be done next week. If you can only do six big things a week, what are the three, maximum four, things you can do a day to achieve this? At first I wrote all six things about work, and my coach told me that's wrong. The six goals must incorporate all aspects of your life, including work, personal, physical and spiritual life. This will result in you being a better delegator as a leader, able to identify what is a priority and what can be tackled next week."

But don't think of your plan as a "to do list." A "to do list" makes it sound like a chore. We prefer to use the term "action list." An action list implies the intention to accomplish something and sounds much more positive.

Tomorrow's action list should be created today. Prioritize and set out what you're going to do tomorrow no later than this evening. Remember to schedule it in a way that works best for you. Think about how your own productivity cycle throughout the day – if you're most alert in the mornings, try getting to the office early; if you focus best after 9:00 p.m., consider creating a less traditional work schedule.

In fact, researchers are paying more and more attention to the topic of chronotypes (your preference for daytime versus nighttime activities, or when you feel most awake and most tired). They've found that the times when people are most creative, energetic and productive vary widely.

Till Roenneberg from Ludwig-Maximilians-Universität in Munich, is one of the leading researchers of chronobiology. A member of an organization called the B-Society, he points out that human beings have a genetically determined circadian rhythm which indicates when a person prefers to be awake and when the preference is for sleep. Our circadian rhythm is genetically determined. It also can change during our life time, as demonstrated by the sleep patterns of the average adolescent, which usually includes sleeping all day, if possible, and staying up all night.

The distribution of circadian rhythms (chronotypes) ranges from people preferring to rise extremely early (early chronotypes) to people preferring to go to bed extremely late (late chronotypes). Individuals with the "early chronotype" are more energetic and productive in the morning and before noon. On the other hand, the "late chronotype" is more energetic in the afternoon and evening. The researchers contend that productivity would dramatically increase if we paid attention to what works best for us and planned our days to be in tune with our most productive cycles.

To make the most of your day, streamline your action list around your highest priorities. Your priorities will vary depending on the stage you're at in your personal life and career, but they'll help you plan your days more effectively and give you more control over how you spend your time. When you plot your action list, focus on the most important tasks. If you find yourself unable to make sense of a confusing tangle of urgent versus important, look at each item and ask yourself, *If I don't get this done, will I be able to sleep tonight?*

Acknowledge what is useful, what is not, and remember to schedule in a little time for interruptions. Inevitably, whether you are in an office environment or even working from home, there will always be interruptions and distractions that can leave you feeling like your day is running away from you and things are getting out of your control. Cushion your action list with the little snippets of time you're likely to lose when you're pulled away from completing your task.

Be aware of who and what pulls you away from the important work you're doing. Negative people who constantly gossip and complain can be a huge drain on your energy. If you can avoid them, do. This isn't being unkind. It is being practical, and poisonous people don't really deserve your precious time. If you can't avoid them, be civil and keep communications and engagement to a minimum.

SMASH IT OUT

Sometimes you don't have the luxury of allowing any interruptions or distractions at all. When you find yourself staring down a monster of a job, put your action list to the side and pull out your "smash-it-out" list. Those things on your action list can be done tomorrow if necessary. The monster has to be dealt with now: your smash-it-out list is a non-negotiable.

If you have just two hours to dedicate to your monster job, know exactly what you need to accomplish in that time and know exactly how you are going to do it. Again, make sure that you plan this the night before, so when you come in the next day, you're finely tuned in to your game plan. Then close the door, turn your phone to silent, focus and execute everything on your smash-it-out list in those two hours. This works as well for the urgent tasks as it does for the big projects. For a bigger project, set aside sections of time every day to dedicate to your smash-it-out list until it's done.

And then of course, there are the things on our action lists that we really don't like to do! If there is something you are dreading, don't spend the whole day worrying about it – make it the first item on your action list instead. You'll be surprised how much energy you create for yourself by getting the most daunting tasks out of the way first.

For some people, those worst tasks are meetings. Meetings are valuable opportunities to communicate, but not all meetings are created equal. Most meetings consume huge amounts of personal and corporate time and often, because they are poorly planned or conducted, they end up wasting the time of those attending. So many of us have to spend half our days in meetings and still need to attend to our "actual" work after all that.

Always be aware of *which* meetings you're so busy scheduling and accepting. People are often far too quick to call a meeting when a simple email or phone call would have sufficed. Tim Ferriss, author of *The 4-Hour Workweek*, says "meetings should only be held to make decisions about a defined problem or situation, not to define the problem." That's when you end up having a meeting about a meeting.

Ferriss also says, "If someone suggests that you meet with them, ask her or him to send you an email with an agenda in order to provide structure to your meeting." This forces people to spell out what they want to achieve from the meeting, and it is often possible to answer the questions by email and without an unnecessary meeting. "If you cannot avoid a meeting, make sure you define the end time," he adds. "Do not leave these discussions open ended; keep them short and prioritize the most important items so you start with those first. If everything is well defined, you should be able to get through your agenda in the time allocated."

A useful tip is to set your phone alarm for the meeting end time. When it rings, just say to the person you are meeting with that you wanted to make sure you honored their time. You don't have to end the meeting abruptly, but it's a good way of bringing it to an end.

Another big time-drainer is email. Most of us start checking our emails first thing, and before we realize it, our top four or five items on our action list quickly become the bottom four or five. We suddenly have so much to do we don't know where to start and we end up wasting precious time. Rather, spend the first 90 minutes of your day completing your first scheduled task. *Then* check your inbox. Now you have a head start on your day, and that always feels good.

Because you can get emails on almost every device you own, learn to set boundaries on when and how often you check your email. Own your technology; don't let it own you. You don't have to jump every time it beeps. If you reply to an email at 8:00 p.m., people will start to expect a response from you no matter what time of the night or day they email you. It can be very unnerving when your phone is pinging the whole day and into the night, reminding you that someone is looking for your attention. One thing you can do right now is remove the email alerts from your phone. Remember that someone else's urgency isn't necessarily yours. As the famous saying goes, "A failure to plan on your part should not constitute an emergency on my part."

In fact, whenever you're doing something that requires your full attention (like something on your smash-it-out list), turn off all automated email, Twitter and Facebook alerts, and silence your phone. University of California, Irvine researchers Gloria Mark and Victor Gonzalez found that it typically takes workers over 20 minutes to resume a task once they've been interrupted. So spare yourself those random interruptions and schedule a few times each day to check and respond to emails, texts and phone calls. That way you'll avoid responding to other people's needs at the expense of your own. And while you are at it, consider introducing technology-free zones into your home, especially at the dinner table. This should be the one hour of the day that is spent truly communicating with the people who are important in your life!

So we've got our action lists, and our smash-it-out lists; we've streamlined our meetings; limited distracting communications; organized our days around our own productive times, and still we feel like there aren't enough hours in the day. What now?

Now we delegate.

As women, even when we have a golden opportunity to delegate, we typically don't. Delegation is one of the most important tools in our kit when it comes to freeing up some valuable time. But, we're committed to and fixated on having it done our way – and if we're honest with ourselves, we also secretly believe that no one will do the job as well as we will.

THE ART OF DELEGATION

A colleague of ours has not-so-fond memories of working at a small college whose administrator insisted on doing everything – an approach that frequently resulted in unnecessary hitches, and sometimes disasters. She was not an effective practitioner of the art of delegation.

If you are going to be an effective and impressive leader, you have to learn to let go and put some faith in the abilities of your colleagues and employees. That doesn't mean you shouldn't be thoughtful and strategic about how you delegate. Instead, you can go about the process artfully by choosing the tasks that you are willing to pass on, selecting the best person for the job, carefully explaining what it is you want done, and being sure to give credit to the individual who takes on the task and does it well.

Rodriguez is referred to as a highly effective time manager because of her art of delegation. She says, "I know what to spend time on and what to delegate. I consider the ROI of my time and constantly look for ways to be more efficient." The art of delegation is to delegate the *right* things. You don't need to be busy. You need to be productive.

In her book *Work Less, Do More*, Jan Yager outlines several key steps to effective delegation:

- First, be strategic about your choice of what to delegate. Use your time and talents to take on the tasks and projects you consider critical, and that you are most capable of completing successfully. As Robin Sharma, world-renowned business leader says, we should outsource or delegate everything we can't be Best in the World at!

- Second, be discriminating about whom you delegate to. Don't choose based on who has the time or will cost the least; rather, take care to delegate the work to those who are most likely to do the job *well*.

- Third, take the time to explain the nature of the task clearly, as well as how you would suggest the task is approached. Keep in mind that it is important to strike a balance between explaining what you expect and respecting the ability of your employees and colleagues to figure out how to get the job done in their own way. Numerous studies have shown that workers who have a sense of autonomy generally perform better than those who are expected to complete a task "by the book."

- Finally, be generous with praise and credit for a job well done. Many people struggle with this step, but the payoffs for positive and well- earned praise are many: people who feel recognized and appreciated are likely to be more loyal to you and your organization, and also likely to be willing to show initiative when the next task comes around.

Letting go is probably the hardest part of delegation. At the end of the day, everyone has their own unique way of approaching a task. Just because it's not your way doesn't mean it's the wrong way. When you do have the opportunity to delegate, remember to give people the power to do it their way. You may even learn something new – or learn a better way. Again, at the root of it all is control. Learn to let go and you could discover amazing things.

OWN YOUR FOCUS

I'm just too busy. There just aren't enough hours in the day. I will never have the time for that. I wish I had more time for myself. Do these sound like familiar thoughts? We lead frenetic, fast-paced lives. With work time, family time and social time all demanding our attention, we're constantly juggling our day-to-day responsibilities and driving ourselves to do all those things we need to do...first for the company, and then for the family, but almost never for ourselves.

When someone else needs our attention, we're quick to cancel that yoga class, the aromatherapy massage we've been looking forward to and even that desperately needed doctor's appointment. We put ourselves last, we suck it up and we get on with it. Michelle Obama is quite outspoken about this, pointing out that "Women in particular need to pay special attention to their mental and physical health, because if we are busy scurrying to and from appointments and errands, we don't have a lot of time to take care of ourselves. We need to do a better job of putting ourselves higher up on our own 'to do' list."

We need to mind ourselves.

We've spoken a lot about choosing to be mindful rather than being mindless, but let's reframe that. Let's choose to be mind-*full*. To be *fully* present and aware.

Research on the benefits of mindfulness reveals that by paying attention to what's going on around us, instead of operating on autopilot, we can reduce stress, unlock creativity, and boost performance both at work and in our personal lives. Practices that help us attain mindfulness, like yoga and meditation, quite literally train the mind and rewire the brain. As a result, three critical things happen: Your ability to concentrate increases, you see things with increasing clarity (which improves your judgment) and you develop level-headedness.

There are so many other advantages to mindfulness. It's easier to pay attention. You remember more of what you've done. You're more creative. You're able to take advantage of opportunities when they present themselves and you can avert difficulties not yet arisen. People even like you better because you're more charismatic and less judgmental. At its simplest, mindfulness is becoming aware of your thoughts in each moment. It's about paying attention to what is going on in your life.

Ellen Langer's research on mindfulness has influenced thinking across several fields, from behavioral economics to positive psychology. She says that mindfulness is the process of actively noticing new things and placing yourself wholly in the present. It's the essence of engagement and makes you more sensitive to context and perspective. And rather than being in an energy-consuming state, mindfulness is actually energizing.

Langer suggests we aim to actively notice five new things every day. This could be anything from what's happening at work to how you look right now. When you keep noticing new things about yourself, your environment and the people in your life, you see options, opportunities and ways of being that you may not have been aware of before.

"Life consists only of moments, nothing more than that," she says. "So if you make the moment matter, it all matters." Wherever you are, be present. When you're at work, actively notice what's going on in the office. When you're at home, pay absolute attention to your family. If you're a working mother, give your children 30 minutes of focused time where you are fully present and undistracted rather than two hours of time divided between your children and your inbox.

Another way to increase your mindfulness is with "micro meditations." Maria Gonzalez, author of the book *Mindful Leadership*, recommends one-to three-minute micro meditations for people who are too busy to meditate. These micro-meditations can be done several times a day for even just one minute at a time. You can do them whenever you feel yourself becoming stressed or overwhelmed, with too much to do and too little time; when you feel distracted and agitated, or even when you're looking for some inspiration.

EXERCISE: THE QUICK AND EASY MICRO-MEDITATION

- **Start by becoming aware of your breath:** Close your eyes and notice your breath. Is your breathing shallow or deep? Are you holding your breath? Tensing your stomach? Clenching your jaw? Or hunching your shoulders?
- **Now start breathing into your belly:** Do not strain. If it feels too unnatural to breathe into the belly, then bring the breath down to the lower chest. If your mind wanders, gently bring your focus back to the breath.
- **Stay with it:** Keep breathing deeply, naturally, rhythmically into your belly, keeping your focus on the breath and allowing your body to relax. Remain in this state for one to three minutes. Gently open your eyes when you are ready.

By practicing this regularly, you will train yourself to become more mindful, calm and focused. You can create reminders for yourself to practice these meditations two to four times a day, every hour or so, or you can also use them on an ad hoc basis whenever you are stressed or need to prepare for a meeting or presentation. Whatever you are doing, micro-meditations can put you back on track and help you develop your mindfulness muscle.

There are two more incredibly important tools to help us develop mindfulness – sleep and exercise.

SLEEP AND EXERCISE

Without enough sleep, we switch to autopilot. Without enough sleep, we cannot be our best selves at work or at home. Without enough sleep, we put our own health on the line. We need to treat bedtime with the same respect and importance we give all our other work-related activities. Have you ever thought about sleep as a meeting you've scheduled with yourself? Arianna Huffington, in her book *Thrive*, says that "too many of us think of sleep as the flexible item in our schedule that can be endlessly moved around to accommodate the "fixed" and top priority of work. But like that flight or train we have to catch, our sleep should be thought of as a fixed point in our day, and everything else should be adjusted so we don't miss it."

Sleep expert Philip Gehrman, PhD, says that functioning on less sleep has almost become a badge of honor, especially in our time-deprived world. However, Gehrman maintains that even if you think you're efficient and productive on less sleep, you're probably not. Studies show that over time, people who are getting six hours of sleep instead of the recommended seven or eight, begin to feel that they've adapted to that sleep deprivation, but the measures taken during tests of mental alertness and performance continue to decline. Gehrman says this means there's a critical point of sleep deprivation when we lose touch with how impaired we really are.

Lack of sleep hurts cognitive processes like thinking and learning. It impairs attention, alertness, concentration, reasoning, and problem-solving. Various sleep cycles also play a role in consolidating memories in the mind, so if you don't get enough sleep, you won't be able to remember what you learned and experienced during the day.

One helpful sleeping tip is to have a warm bath or shower before you go to bed and keep your bedroom cool. Because your body temperature drops when you sleep, keeping your room cooler helps improve the quality of your rest.

If sleep doesn't come easily to you, try a little exercise. According to a study published in the *Mental Health and Physical Activity* journal, people sleep significantly better and feel more alert during the day if they get at least 150 minutes of exercise a week. Exercise is another one of those things we quickly brush off our lists whenever something "more important" comes up. We know exercise is good for us, and we might intend to get around to it at least three times a week, but somehow the week slips away and we haven't even managed five minutes. And, no, walking to the coffee machine does not count as exercise.

Melissa Dawn Simkins is a fervent proponent of making time for exercise. "There is a connection between being successful and caring for your body," she says. "Getting up in the morning to work out sometimes feels challenging, but when you follow through with it, you start to establish an 'I can defeat this' attitude."

Exercise is not just for those who want to look good in the mirror or squeeze into a smaller dress size. Exercise is for everyone who wants to feel more confident, de-stress and function at their optimum, both physically and mentally. And, just as you should schedule your sleep like it's a meeting, so you should schedule your exercise.

Some people thrive on exercise more than others. You don't have to run a marathon; find something that works for you. Change your attitude on how you view exercise. It's not a punishment; it is a way to reconnect with yourself. Find physical activity you enjoy, whether it's walking, swimming, dancing, hiking, or tennis. If you need a friend to motivate you, team up with someone you can have fun with. If you need a personal trainer to keep you going, find a trainer who can inspire you. If you decide to brave a group class at the gym, make sure you stand next to the strongest person for some additional inspiration. If you don't have time before or after work, make your exercise a lunch date instead, even if you just step out for 20 minutes to walk around the block. Research shows that workers who take time for exercise on a regular basis are more productive and have more energy than their more inactive colleagues.

And there's one last thing you absolutely have to schedule into your diary. Me time.

ME TIME

We're smart. We all instinctively know that when we take time for ourselves to pursue our passions, to do the things that we enjoy, to relax, or even to do nothing at all, we end up happier, healthier and feeling better. *Me time* allows us to de-stress, unwind and rejuvenate. Yes, we know this in theory, but when it comes to actually implementing a little "me time," we're not very successful.

As women, we're always making time for everyone else, but we feel guilty about making time for ourselves. But me time is something you should never feel guilty about. It's nothing more than treating yourself to an activity you enjoy. The world isn't suddenly going to fall apart when you take a little time out. In fact, it's the other way around. Women who never allow themselves their own space often wind up feeling frustrated, tired, overwhelmed, and out of balance... and that's when things start to fall apart.

"We have become overly attached to our busyness," says life strategist Jenni Trent Hughes. "Busy and stressed have somehow become inextricably linked with success, so if you're not busy or stressed then you must not be doing enough."

Decide that you deserve some sacred time each day. Give yourself permission to relax, refocus and recharge. When you're rejuvenated, you can return to your responsibilities with greater focus, commitment and enjoyment. Whether it's taking a long bath, doing something creative or simply reading your favorite book, you need to reconnect with yourself and give yourself time to reflect on your own goals and achievements.

So plan your personal time and have the discipline to stick to the plan. At the beginning of each week, designate specific me time slots of 15 to 20 minutes every day, and treat it like you would any other appointment: make it a non-negotiable.

Decide how you most want to spend that me time. It can be something (or nothing) that allows you to be alone with your thoughts and helps you to release your mind and all those responsibilities. If you had an extra 15 minutes, 30 minutes, an afternoon, or an entire day, what would you do to make yourself feel rejuvenated, relaxed and happy? How each of us chooses to spend free time is as individualized as we are. Write your own list and keep it handy when you begin scheduling time into your calendar.

In an incredibly moving campaign called #LetGo by Sanctuary Spa in the UK, Jenni Trent Hughes urges us to "Get present to your presence." "Take a long hard look at yourself," she says. "Is there a sparkle in your eye? Is there still a slight skip in your step? How often do you find yourself laughing at absolutely nothing? If you met yourself at a party would you think, *Oh I'd like to be friends with her!* If you don't like the answers to those questions, then maybe it's time for a rethink "

We recommend you go and watch the video at www.sanctuary.com/en-gb/letgo.

When you make it a top priority, you'll find that you can gain some time for yourself. And, you'll be amazed at how those little pockets of *me time* can make a huge difference in your health and happiness! Remember you need to make a decision to own your time or someone else will happily own it for you.

OWN YOUR TIME ... IN A FLASH

- Let go of perfectionism; have the courage to be imperfect.
- Instead of focusing on work-life balance, see the two parts as a whole and focus on work-life integration.
- Learn to say no, and use the Yes Sandwich as a gracious way out.
- Plan your day the night before.

- Schedule everything, including sleep, exercise and *me time*.
- Create action lists for your top priorities and smash-it-out lists for the tasks that matter most.
- Complete your first scheduled task of the day before you check your inbox.
- Decline meetings when a phone call or email communication will suffice.
- Learn to let go and delegate.
- Be fully present, whether you're at work or at home. Fully engage with the people around you.
- Build in daily pockets of me time to reconnect with yourself.

6 Own
YOUR NETWORK

The richest people in the world look for and build networks. Everyone else looks for work.

—ROBERT KIYOSAKI

Almost all of the women we meet in our workshops or interviewed for this book, and almost every accomplished person you'll ever meet, owe their success in some part to the people in their networks. People who've helped them along the way.

Take a moment to think about all the people in your life who have assisted you in getting to where you are right now. Then think about those *you* have assisted, people whose lives you have directly impacted because you gave them a chance or introduced them to the right person. The people in our networks could start as friends and family, but as we grow our networks and move along our career paths, they'll also be connections that we develop at work, online, on our travels, at social events, and through exploring hobbies or outside interests.

Have you ever thought about actively growing your network? What if you were to expand your network by just a few people – what impact would that have? To own your network, to really work your network, you need to strengthen your current relationships within your existing network, look for ways to expand and develop new ones, and continually work on building real, meaningful, reciprocal relationships.

In order to fine-tune our networking skills, we all need to enhance our ability to do three key things: connect, converse and collaborate. Edith Venter freely acknowledges that the keys to her success are the contacts that she's made over the years. She works at it, though. She continually nurtures those contacts, never damages relationships, never closes doors in ways that they can't be knocked on again, and always treats her contacts with respect.

"The higher you go up the corporate ladder, the less the job is about you and the more it is about the people you know," says author Becky Blalock.

As a pioneer in the travel industry, Joanna Mukoki truly understands the power of connections. She says that networking is incredibly important in the corporate environment where "doors open because you knew somebody who knew somebody." She always attends the key events, and she's good at making and maintaining relationships because she makes it easy. "When you meet someone and you get a business card and you feel like there is a connection, then take them out for coffee. You'll be surprised at what you can learn," Mukoki says. "I travel a lot internationally and I am present at every moment. Every experience is part of the journey. I talk to people even before I board my flight. In being present, you'll be amazed at what you learn about yourself and what networks you can build around yourself."

OWN THE CONNECTION

The old hierarchies in the workplace are disappearing, and, in their place, people are developing diverse, widespread networks that transcend generational, cultural and social differences – networks that are becoming the key social structure for efficiency, creativity and progress. Your social network could help you open doors, get access to hard-to-obtain information, build business resources, and even secure career sponsorships.

Carolyn Jackson points out that it's still unusual for a female to get invited to a male CEO's house for weekend meetings. To combat this, she says, "do something else they like doing. So, it's not necessarily coming over to the house, but if they like fly fishing or golf, you have to go." More women are heeding this advice, with golf and other sports pros teaching women how to play the game as well as how to close those important deals that are often made on the golf course.

If networking sounds like it could involve a little work, it does. And it's not the kind of work you can bill by the hour, either. But, it's something that can heighten your socio-economic status; boost your authority, your career, and your pay stub; and give you the support you need.

EXERCISE: ASSESS YOUR LEVEL OF NETWORK OWNERSHIP

Grab a piece of paper and a pen, and write down your answers to the following questions:

- You have a choice between attending a party or staying home and watching the latest episode of your favorite TV show. What do you choose?
- You receive an invitation to a cocktail party honoring a long- time employee who is about to retire. What is your response?
- You are attending a convention that will feature presentations on the latest research in your field. The schedule includes a "mixer" before the presentation. How excited are you about this mixer?
- Do you play any team sports for fun? If so, which one(s)?
- Do you belong to any volunteer organizations? If so, which one(s)?
- Do you want to make more connections with people in your work and social environment, but you don't know how to start going about it?

Take a moment to assess your answers. Do your answers reveal you as a person who'll make the most of every opportunity to build a stronger network or someone who will shy away from it? Or are you a little bit of both?

For some people, networking at an event and having conversations with strangers comes totally naturally. Others would much rather stay home or keep to their hotel rooms than participate in any kind of social or work event. Networking isn't impossible for those of us who are a little more introverted than others. We need to play to our strengths in everything we do, and that includes how we choose to network.

Socializing and networking may not be something you find effortless, but like a muscle, the more you use it, the stronger it gets. And don't think that you are the only uncomfortable one there. It may be reassuring to know that so many other people feel exactly like you do. People who experience shyness, and feel nervous or anxious in the company of others often fear negative judgment. Some people even feel anxious about greeting someone new because they're imagining the conversation petering out awkwardly before it's even started. If any of this sounds familiar, work with some of the tools in our earlier chapters – like Amy Cuddy's two-minute power pose (Chapter 2) – and remember to give yourself permission to be there; remember that you have as much right as anyone else to be there.

As with most things in life, when it comes to making connections, it's often easier to start small. Your social presence shouldn't only be reserved for the people you perceive to be the higher-ups and the influencers. Start with your workmates and contemporaries, the people who share your daily working experience. Depending on where you are in your career, these people may not be very influential right now, but they may very well become the ones with all the influence in the years to come.

Ask yourself, right now, what kind of relationship you have with the people you work with every day. When you're making work connections, you're not necessarily making friends; you don't have to be best buddies to form a meaningful bond with another person. Just be interested enough to care. Do you know what their biggest challenges are? Do you ever offer to get them a cup of coffee or suggest going out for lunch together? Make a point of sharing information with your colleagues. If you come across an opportunity that you think would be appropriate for someone you know at work, share it. We guarantee that if you go out of your way to be a resource to your colleagues, your generosity will, in most cases, be repaid many times over.

It's also important to expose yourself to as many different environments as possible, particularly where there are opportunities to connect. Once you've gained confidence within your network amongst your peers, widen your interpersonal horizons. Volunteer – both in your personal and your work environment. This is a great way to increase your visibility. Join a sports team, book club or religious group. Think as broadly as possible, because there are more ways than one to gain access to those important individuals who can give you support and help further your career.

Take advantage of all of those work-related social events that come your way and look for groups or associations that are relevant to your area of interest. For example, if you are in sales and marketing, you could join a local or international marketing association. Chances are there'll be an active group close to where you live. You may also want to explore online groups within your area of expertise.

People do business with those they like and trust. If you have strong relationships, you can get far more done, and you'll likely be given access to more information and opportunities through your networks. What will take you years to achieve individually can happen so much more quickly if you talk to the right people. In addition, you'll get so much value *yourself* from serving as a resource and helping others succeed. This is a value women really need to leverage. For many men, networking is like second nature. They easily structure their interactions and can identify where to find what they need. However, many women require a more purposeful approach to networking. We also tend to view our other responsibilities as more important, so networking gets pushed to the bottom of the to do list. At the same time, there are mixed perceptions about women who more actively put themselves out there, and this concerns a lot of us. But networking is powerful, so we need to be better and more intentional about it.

If you're one of those people who would rather go for a root canal than attend a networking event filled with strangers, here are some pointers that could make the process a lot less painful – and hopefully much more productive.

First, create an agenda for the event. What do you hope to accomplish from attending this event? Try to come up with a few specific goals. For example, you could set the goal of introducing yourself to three new people. It will help you walk through the door with a sense of purpose. Even better, specify what sort of people you want to meet (perhaps it's even one particular person) and specify what you'd like to learn from them.

Working towards a goal doesn't mean you won't be able to enjoy yourself. In fact, going in with a clear goal can work wonders for your confidence. Once you know with whom you want to connect and why, you will feel less like you're hanging onto a loose end. Of course, you still have to start a conversation with a complete stranger, but whether you're shy, introverted or a seasoned networker, whether you're amongst your peers, industry leaders or at a social event, starting a conversation anytime, anywhere, can be much easier than you think.

You can start a conversation with a comment about anything that genuinely interests you, from the latest industry news to the decor or the food they're serving. You could give a compliment about the person's necklace or tie. You could express your admiration for one of the speakers at the event or even lightly knock the traffic you got stuck in on your way there. In most cases, unless they are extremely busy or distracted, the other party will respond, and so the conversation begins. Remember to bring your mindfulness into the situation. Stop overthinking things, forget about how you look or what you might say next. Rather, pay attention and listen.

If you initiate a conversation and that particular group of people doesn't seem to want an additional member, don't take it personally. They may simply be a group of friends who are more interested in catching up with each other than meeting new people at the moment. One of the biggest mistakes people make at networking events is to persist in trying to interact when it is clear the best course of action is to let it go and move on.

If you're really anxious to make contact with a certain member in that group, wait until they've left the group or until you sense from their body language that the group is now welcoming new members. How can you tell? You don't want to stare, but you can make some discrete observations, such as noticing whether the group has physically opened up. Have people moved apart? Do the members of this group appear to have turned their attention away from each other? Is there a lull in the conversation?

If you happen to be nearby, the group might invite you to join them. If not, you can use a line like, "I couldn't help but overhear..." Yes, it's a bit of a cliché, but its intent is easily recognizable and will signal your interest in joining.

If you can't seem to break into groups, it is perfectly fine to approach people who are standing alone. This might actually be the preferred technique if you need to speak with someone in particular because you'll have their full attention.

Once you've broken the ice, you need to keep the conversation going and here's where your skill for meaningful conversation will help you solidify the relationship with your new connection. Bring to mind the advice of Dale Carnegie, who famously characterized people who talk about themselves as bores, people who talk about others as gossips, and people who talk about you as brilliant conversationalists. If you find yourself at a loss for something to talk about, remember that people are normally quite happy to talk about themselves. You can get the ball rolling by asking them about the various phases of their lives: their past, present and future. You can ask where they went to school or when they first knew they were interested in a particular career. Current questions can include asking what their greatest challenges are or what they like most or least about their job. When asking about their future, you can ask about their career aspirations or their plans for their next holiday.

Of course it also helps to do a little homework first. Become familiar with some of the most recent developments involving the companies of the people you aim to connect with. With a little background knowledge, you could ask about the particular challenges facing the company or make observations about its recent developments.

Don't overstay your welcome in a conversation. Once you have accomplished your goal, like arranging an appointment or making an introduction, you can leave. Don't do so abruptly, of course. Rather, ease your way out politely and move on. Once awkward pauses start cropping up in a conversation, it's generally time to bring things to a close. The goal of these events is to make contact with many people, and you won't reach your goal if you glue yourself to someone's side or allow others to glue themselves to yours.

Keep in mind that everybody has the same goal as you, so when someone signals they're ready to move on, don't feel rejected.

Try out conversation tactics and the networking advice that works for you at every event you attend. But most of all, focus on being genuine. People can spot a lack of authenticity. If you're talking to someone and trying to pretend you're fascinated by what they're saying when you're not, you'll come off as insincere. Be honest about the fact that you are attending this event because you want to get something out of it – just like everyone else. You are there to find resourceful people, not to make lifelong friends. That's what these events are for, and everybody's fine with it.

Sue Shellenbarger, who writes about careers for *The Wall Street Journal*, advises:

- Don't measure success by the number of business cards you collect.
- Don't look over the shoulder of the person you're talking to in case someone more interesting shows up.

- Don't try to look smarter and more competent than others so people will be drawn to you.
- Don't assume anyone standing alone is a loser and should be avoided.
- Don't demonstrate your power and influence by talking in a loud voice.

One of the qualities that is off-putting when initiating contact is neediness. Don't ever go into a conversation with a sense of desperation, especially when you're attempting to build relationships with people you perceive to have more power or influence than yourself. Approach the encounter with the attitude that you and the other person are on a level playing field. Even if they outrank you, you still have a great deal to offer and you deserve equal consideration.

But even when you're comfortable conversing with people more influential than you, it can still be quite a challenge just to gain access to those top executives. Nothing is impossible, though – all you need to do is apply the tools of targeted networking.

CONNECTING WITH KEY PLAYERS USING TARGETED NETWORKING

The first step in targeted networking is to identify the person with whom you need to connect. This may sound obvious, but we often find that people neglect to identify the key players who can help them make a career move or a business connection – even in cases that simply involve another department within the same company. Once you know who you want to reach, you can develop the most effective approach to get access.

This strategy might need a little lateral thinking on your part. Let's say you'd like to be hired by a particular company to present training programs. Your first thought might be to find a way to meet the CEO, but the more appropriate person to speak to would be the Head of Human Resources or Head of Training. Using a platform like LinkedIn, you should find it easy enough to identify who the Head of Human Resources is. Once you know who they are, you could call their assistant and try to set up a meeting.

An even more efficient approach would be to find out if anyone in your existing network knows the Head of Human Resources personally. Using that tactic, you might very well find out that you are already connected to several people who work for HR within the company. This is where your social presence and networking expertise come in. Now you can contact these people and ask their advice on the best way to set up a meeting with the decision-maker.

Never demand an introduction. Never *expect* an introduction. Introductions to the higher-ups are a privilege, not a right, and if you take an entitled approach with your contact, you might just annihilate your chances of success.

A request is always much more effective. For example, you could say the following: "You have been so successful in navigating your career at Company X. I am hoping to meet with your Head of HR. Do you have any advice as to the best way to proceed?" Hopefully, your contact will volunteer an introduction, which means you already have the advantage. Then, thank them in a way that validates the contribution. This way they'll feel good about helping you out and will be more open to supporting you again in the future.

Use every resource at your disposal for targeted networking, including social media. By now you should realize there are platforms that are much more than just forums to post your CV and look for a job.

TAP INTO THE POWER OF THE ONLINE SPACE

Never underestimate the power of social media for taking your networking abilities up a notch. For example, did you know that you can ask for introductions on LinkedIn? In fact, as a social networking site specifically geared towards the business community, and which has a worldwide reach, LinkedIn is one of the most critical online tools in strategically building and nurturing relationships.

There are three degrees of connections on LinkedIn: people you're directly connected to (first-degree connections); people who are connected to your first-degree connections (these are your second- degree connections); and finally, people who are connected to your second-degree connections. If, in your targeted networking, you find that the person you'd like to reach out to is connected to one of your first-degree connections on LinkedIn, you can ask your first-degree contact to connect the two of you.

If you choose to go this route, don't just send a generic request. Take the time to write a clear message, and give a persuasive reason for an introduction that would ultimately benefit all parties.

People also greatly underestimate the professional value that Twitter offers. In your targeted networking attempts, you may not be able to find an email address for the person you want to connect with, but you're likely to find them on Twitter. Don't be afraid to tweet them. Start a relationship with this person online by following them, or commenting on or retweeting their posts.

You might also be surprised at what you find in your old emails. Instead of leaving them lying there dormant, go through them and see what contacts you can rekindle. Organize your inbox and archives to rediscover these potential contacts — even check your sent items. The smallest thing, like an old press release or newsletter you once filed, could provide the connection to a firm or business you're now interested in. By going through old emails, you may even find out that half the initial legwork is already done.

And don't ever be afraid to cold-email someone you want to get to know. When you have their professional information and career highlights (thank you, Google), it makes it so much easier to create an authentic interaction, even if you haven't met them yet. Email, ask questions and set up a meeting for coffee.

But don't overdo it. Be genuine, be credible and be visible. Take your time. Once you've built a relationship online, you can take the next step by taking it into the real world. Learn to use the power of networking to turn those virtual connections into real relationships offline.

GIVE BEFORE YOU TAKE

There are three key phases of the relationship-building process. The first two are connection and conversation. The third is collaboration. You're much more likely to develop important contacts and career connections if you show people you're not always on the take. Show people you're also generous with your time, advice and guidance. Show that you're not just a go-getter, but you're a go-giver, too.

Build relationships with a diverse array of people. Don't concern yourself with whether or not these people can help you with your career right at this moment, because you might find that they will fulfill a different role in your life in the future.

And make it clear that you don't expect favors from them. You'll be surprised at how much more open and receptive people are when they don't feel like they're about to be extorted. Social networks are defined as being mutually reciprocal relationships, and people with the best social presence understand that networking is often more about "What can I do for you?" than it is about "What can you do for me?" As Jackson says, "If I could even get an audience with a decision maker, it was about being smart, showing my capability, and offering to do anything they needed done."

Make a point of remembering people's birthdays, including staff and clients, and without being nosy, make sure you know something about their lives outside the office. Keep lists of people based on location, so you can look up the people you know and email them or send them a relevant article.

In the iconic book, *How to Win Friends and Influence People*, Dale Carnegie writes, "You can make more friends in two months by becoming interested in other people than you can in two years by trying to get other people interested in you." And Lynne Waymon, co-author of the book *Make Your Contacts Count*, says that networking is about "teaching and giving – teaching people about who you are, what to come to you for, what you're good at, what they can count on you for. And then it's about listening so generously so that you can help other people get what they need."

So, be generous. Exchange ideas, resources and contacts. Give your time, your guidance and your advice. If you're in the early stages of your career and you're wondering what exactly you are in a position to give, remember that giving comes in many forms. Exchange skills, expertise and talents with your peers to help them get one of their ideas off the ground, to launch a new project together or even help them get a job.

If your writing and editing skills are strong, you could offer to proofread their resumes. It may not sound like much to you, but resumes are often littered with typos, poor grammar, text talk, and, yes, even emoticons. Poorly presented resumes tend to nosedive straight into the recycle bin, so your proofreading could make all the difference in the world to someone looking for a job.

If you're the kind of person who naturally uplifts and inspires those around her, be there for people when they need a little motivation or support. They'll always remember you for it. If you're a good listener, listen. Most often, people just need to be heard. When you believe in someone, tell them. A little external affirmation is a great boost for anyone climbing the ladder to success. It's so often the little things that count, like support, encouragement, belief, kindness, acknowledgment and respect. These are things you can give freely, no matter who you are or where you happen to be in your career. What you are building is relationship capital, which is effectively a long-term investment that will hold you through the good and the bad.

Collaboration is the essence of sustained networking, and it depends on an on-going attitude of mutual reciprocity. If you want to remain connected with the people you meet, you have to work at it. It doesn't happen magically.

Maintaining relationships requires specific, sustained effort, and the more thoughtful you can be, the more memorable you will become.

BUILD BRIDGES WITH FOLLOW-UP

Once you have made your all-important connections at those networking events, at work or at social functions, the next step is to incorporate your new contacts into your network. Exchange contact information...and then follow up. Networking provides the connection, but follow-ups provide the bridge. Without the bridge, you cannot advance the relationship to the next level. A contact you don't follow up on is a contact who will never become a part of your network.

Start and maintain a database of the contacts in your network. List names, email addresses, phone numbers, as well as how, when and where you met. Include any other pertinent notes that could help jar your memory and spark ideas for collaborating and giving. If, during your conversation you picked up on someone's particular area of interest, send them an article or a book suggestion related to that interest.

Then keep adding to your database. Build profiles. Include as much relevant detail as you can. Make a point of keeping in touch with your connections by sending appropriate news or information. The next time you hear of a spectacular career move by an executive you want to impress, write a congratulatory note on reaching the next phase of an extraordinary career.

And when you feel ready, when your objective is clear, when you have something to offer as much as you have something you'd like to gain, never be afraid to ask for that coffee meeting.

FIND A SPONSOR

You might be lucky enough to have a mentor, but have you ever thought about getting a sponsor too? There's a big difference between a mentor and a sponsor. According to Sylvia Ann Hewlett, author of *Forget a Mentor, Find a Sponsor*, "Mentors act as a sounding board or a shoulder to cry on, offering advice as needed, and support and guidance as requested; they expect very little in return. Sponsors, in contrast, are much more vested in their protégés, offering guidance and critical feedback because they believe in them." In other words, Hewlett says, "sponsors are powerful people who can really open doors for you."

Sponsorship isn't just for people who are employed in the corporate world. Sponsorship applies to entrepreneurs as well. The basic principle of sponsorship is about finding someone who can open doors that you wouldn't be able to access on your own. Entrepreneurs can look within fields complementary to their own, or even in completely different industries for influential sponsors who can make introductions to potential clients, investors or people who could offer media exposure.

Without a sponsor, Hewlett warns that we risk getting stuck in the sticky middle slice of management known as the "marzipan layer," where so many driven and talented women find themselves stalling.

Bonnie Marcus calls sponsorship your Get out of Jail Free Card. She's the author of *The Politics of Promotion: How High-Achieving Women Get Ahead and Stay Ahead*, and says that just as a Get out of Jail Free Card in the game of *Monopoly* gets you out of tough situations and propels you forward, so a sponsor is in the prime position to protect you and promote you to win in the workplace.

Getting a sponsor is definitely worth thinking about. You need someone who has the power to push you through the system. Women have a tendency to seek out role models or people they admire, rather than those with the power to take action on their behalf. Instead of only seeking out *role models*, look for people at the senior leadership level who have both the respect in the organization and the clout to make things happen for you.

But you can't just walk up to someone and ask for a sponsorship. Like anything worth attaining, sponsorship is something you have to work for. It's a form of targeted networking that requires you to really hone in on who is who at a company, and who you feel wields the power to help you accelerate your career.

So, how do you approach this incredibly impressive and powerful person who could change the trajectory of your entire career? You can start by thinking about what will make a difference to the company and then selling your ideas to one of the managers. You could tell them, for example, "I know this is outside my job description, but I have identified some solutions for cost savings and process improvements. Would you support me? I would like to bring something additional to the table." At the end of the day, this shows ownership, and that in turn demonstrates your commitment to the company and your potential for successfully taking on greater responsibilities.

Consistently prove you're a hard worker and that you have what it takes to progress. Show your prospective sponsor that you have a proven track record, so they feel confident enough to recommend you for opportunities. You cannot hope that others will somehow find out about your successes; you need to take the initiative to make sure the right people know who you are and that they know what you're doing (we've got some really effective tools for this in Chapter 7).

Another way you can identify someone who could be a great sponsor is by engaging with them as a mentor first. There is a fundamental difference between the relationship dynamics when it comes to mentors and sponsors. With a mentor, you're free to ask for support and guidance fairly early on in the relationship since they're not risking anything to help you. With a sponsor, however, you need to be subtler and develop a relationship over time.

Once you've developed a solid rapport with your mentor, and you've proven your skills and abilities, the relationship can move into more of a sponsorship dynamic. You always need to demonstrate your competence and reliability. Maintain absolute integrity and deliver on what you promised – and do it on time. It can be the difference between moving forward and standing still. It also shows your loyalty to your sponsor. Don't ever forget that by backing you and putting you forward for certain roles and responsibilities, your sponsor is putting their reputation and credibility on the line. In order to have a successful sponsor relationship, you need to prove your loyalty, your capabilities and your trustworthiness. Be patient. It's a relationship that's built project by project, and takes a lot of finessing.

The essential principle of sponsorship is collaboration and making yourself valuable. As with networking, sponsorships are mutually beneficial relationships, so make sure you're not entirely focused on what's in it for you. Give before you take, and you'll start creating mutually beneficial relationships.

OWN YOUR NETWORK...IN A FLASH

- Strengthen your current relationships and find opportunities to develop new ones.
- Build meaningful, reciprocal relationships with people both personally and professionally.
- Be the collaborator; ask, "What can I do for you?"
- Have clear networking goals, identify the people with whom you need to connect, and be prepared with questions as well as answers.
- Don't overstay your welcome during a networking encounter, and if you're rejected, don't take it personally.
- Be genuine, and be genuinely interested.
- Utilize the power of social media and email for maintaining relationships with targeted connections.
- Follow up on the contacts you make. Keep in touch, make that coffee date.
- Maintain a database of the contacts in your network.
- Have mentors, but ensure you find a sponsor, too.

7 Own
YOUR DECISIONS, SUCCESSES, FAILURES, AND FINANCES

When you take risks you learn that there will be times when you succeed and there will be times when you fail, and both are equally important.

— ELLEN DEGENERES

OWN YOUR DECISIONS

Think about all the decisions we are faced with every day. From the moment we wake up, our day is filled with hundreds of decisions, some big and some small: what to eat for breakfast, which belt will go with which shoes, which profile picture to put on Facebook, whom to follow on Twitter, which restaurant to go to, which movie to see, which book to read. And then there are the life-changing decisions: which house to buy, whether or not to have children, where to send those children to school, whether or not to take that job in another city, how to deal with complex family dynamics.

Whether it's the culmination of daily decisions, or that one big decision that has the potential to be life-changing, all the choices we make have consequences. Sometimes our decisions lead to success. Other times those decisions can lead to a less-than-ideal outcome, even failure.

And we all know how terrifying the thought of failure can be.

Failure can be a dark, frustrating, humiliating place that most of us will do anything to avoid. For some of us, that even means not making any decisions at all. We might even convince ourselves we're simply being incredibly thorough when we're over-analyzing every conceivable angle, but sometimes all we are doing is stalling. We are paralyzed with the fear of making the wrong decision.

How would you rate your decision-making skills? In an analysis of several hundred people who had accumulated fortunes well beyond the million-dollar mark, Napoleon Hill, author of *Think and Grow Rich*, writes that every one of those successful people had the habit of reaching decisions promptly, and of changing their decisions slowly – if they changed them at all. He goes on to say that people who fail to accumulate money, without exception, have the habit of reaching decisions very slowly, if at all, and of changing these decisions quickly and often.

So, which category do you fit into?

Indecision is not just an agonizing place to be; it's utterly disempowering. When we're faced with a choice, we need to make a decision. Then, we need to own that decision completely. And the first step toward owning our decisions is to accept the imperfection of life, and to accept that roadblocks and failures are inevitable.

At some time, everybody fails at something. It's unreasonable to think that absolutely everything we're ever going to touch will turn to proverbial gold. So, yes, sometimes we are going to fail. And we need to own our failures as much as we own our successes. What if we could shift our mindset and start to see setbacks, not as negatives, but as opportunities to improve?

The reality is that failure doesn't have to be permanent. It only becomes permanent if we don't take action. If you have ever watched babies who are learning to walk for the first time, you have observed that they are experts at falling down, even crying for a few moments and then getting right back up again. You never see them fall, cry and then give up. While we all did this instinctively as infants, as adults we sometimes forget to have a good cry and then get up again.

"Just keep trying," says Cynthia Good. "You have a good cry, you take a deep breath, and you go back out there and do the best you can. Because we women are so hard on ourselves and hold ourselves to such a high standard, it's important to remember that emotional health requires you to be kind and gentle to yourself."

Resilience – the ability to persevere again after setbacks – is the one thing that all individuals who have achieved even a modicum of success have in common. They bounce back from disappointments. The one thing Nelson Mandela, Mahatma Gandhi, Steve Jobs, and Oprah Winfrey all have in common is the ability to cope with the challenges that came their way.

Think about where you are at right now. Are you allowing a setback to sabotage you, or are you looking at all the ways you can take action, treating the setback as an opportunity rather than a failure? We know this is easier said than done, but as we have said countless times in this book, so much of the way we feel about a situation depends on our mindset, and knowing we are not alone can be a great source of comfort.

Shakespeare put it perfectly when he wrote, "For there is nothing either good or bad, but thinking makes it so."

When it comes to decision-making, is your thinking helping or hurting you? On a scale of one to ten, how do you rate your confidence when it comes to making decisions? A ten would be approaching your decision in a calculated and thoughtful way. You know that there's no perfect decision, but you make it anyway; you move on and accept the consequences. A one is becoming completely inert and paralyzed by the fear that the decision you make won't be perfect, so you don't make one at all, or you let others make it for you.

We are not going to overcome the fear of making the wrong choice until we realize that there is no such thing as perfection. No single decision is perfect. Nobody ever makes the correct choice 100% of the time. Every choice we make comes with a set of consequences. And when we make those choices, we need to take action; we need to hold ourselves accountable, and, most importantly, we need to learn to trust ourselves.

We also need to remind ourselves that we made the best decision at the time, given the information we had. In some cases, the information can come from deep within you, in the form of intuition. We very often hesitate to listen to our intuitive wisdom because we've been taught that it's something irrational. But it's not. Intuitive wisdom, or instinct, is actually the product of the knowledge gained from our life experiences. It helps us to understand what actions are likely to be the most (and the least) beneficial for us, even when we don't have an excess of data or when the facts don't clearly support one action over another. For example, instinct is what allows us to sense whether a person is trustworthy or not. It's a mental shortcut that allows us to gain clarity about a decision or a situation without the need to agonize over every detail.

If you're trying to make a decision and one option doesn't seem right, but you can't put your finger on what exactly it is about that choice that's worrying you, it's probably your instinct pointing you in a healthier direction. If there's something about an action you're planning to take that just doesn't sit well and it keeps nagging at you, then it probably isn't the best choice. Likewise, if you notice yourself getting excited when you think about taking a particular action – even if that action seems to be coming out of left field or isn't seen as the most logical decision on paper – you might want to acknowledge that feeling. It could turn out to be an amazing opportunity for you. And if you are really stuck, ask yourself what you would tell your best friend to do. When you take away the personal aspect of it and take a step back, it is easier to assess the situation. Be aware of thoughts such as *I should, I must* and *I ought to*. Remember these Mind Sneakers (from Chapters 1 and 5) that hamper effective decision-making. When these thoughts appear, try reverting to the technique of asking yourself what you would tell your best friend to do.

And, speaking of best friends, you might want to check in with mentors and advisors. That's what Amy Kleinhans-Curd does. "When it comes to big decisions, I often have an immediate gut feel for what I would want to do," she says, "but I am very aware of the fact that every action has a ripple effect on the world around me. I have a network of mentors and advisors I consult, which I often find edifying as it adds to the quality and richness of the decision. Getting others' perspective is of vital importance, as it helps to expand my awareness of how it will affect those around me; it also gives me a great idea for troubleshooting before the decision is made."

Another key factor in making decisions is knowing what it is you really want, as this will influence the choices you make. Ben Hunt-Davis was on the Olympic rowing team for nine years, and he wrote a book called *Will It Make the Boat Go*

Faster? The book is based on his experiences with his rowing team. They were continually pulling in average results during competitions, until eventually, the members of the team decided to change their thinking and create a new benchmark for making decisions.

In a video on his website, Hunt-Davis shares: "In sport, the temptation is to think that it's about getting it right on the day but it's all about what happens leading up to the big day...We realized that if we continued to do what we've always done, we would continue to get the same results." The team made the choice to change. Before embarking on any task – whether it was during training or elsewhere – they would ask themselves the question: *Will it make the boat go faster?* With this question in mind, the team members refocused their thinking and determined how to approach their goal.

Having a focus and a goal will go a long way towards streamlining your decision-making process and removing much of the uncertainty.

Another decision-making tool is to pose the worst-case scenario question. Most of the time, our anticipated worst-case scenario never transpires. But if you feel that the consequences of the worst outcome are unbearable, then it's probably not the path for you. It's about knowing the difference between negative outcomes that seem worse in your mind (because they're exaggerated by your fear of making a "wrong" choice) and those negative consequences that you truly can't live with.

Always be aware that fear of a situation is based on previous experiences; it is a memory, rather than a future prediction. Feelings are only based in the present and past tense. In fact, one of our workshop participants once said FEAR stands for False Events Appearing Real, and this is very often true.

Making productive decisions is also about being as prepared as possible. If you're considering a new position, have you researched the company? Who would you be working for? What would the role entail? There is great power in knowledge, and having all the information will help you to make a far more informed decision. You could also use the old, reliable method of taking out a pen and paper and writing down the pros and cons. When you have something on paper, it becomes more tangible and allows you to weigh the significance of going with a particular option. If your pros column completely outweighs the cons, then you have your answer.

What if you've exhausted all the options? If you have already listed the pros and cons, tuned in to your intuitive response, as well as assessed the worst-case scenario, and you *still* can't make a decision, then consider taking a test drive for a limited amount of time.

Say, for example, you want to start a new business or you want to see how you'd enjoy a different position within your company and you're unsure about whether or not it'll be a good move for you. Try it out. Test the waters. Tell yourself you'll give it a go for six months, then make sure you give it your best and do everything you can to determine whether it's a good fit. If, after the six-month period, you're not happy with your choice or it's not working out as you had envisioned, then at least you know you gave it your best shot.

Whatever your decision is, once you've made it, go for it. Don't wait for the perfect time (remember – perfect doesn't exist). We're experts at convincing ourselves that we can't go ahead with something because of external factors. But the reality for so many of us is that we'll always be able find some kind of excuse as to why we shouldn't take that leap. If we let it stop us, we will never push ourselves to do anything. If the timing isn't perfect, ask yourself if you can find a way to make it work anyway. And do you know what? You probably can. One of our favorite mottos is that you don't need to know what the end looks like in order to start. Trust your instinct and go for it.

So go ahead and press the start button. Avoid the what if trap and accept what is. Don't wonder about what could have been. Once a decision is made, commit to it and own it. That way you can reap the rewards of being fully invested.

Former Religious Freedom Ambassador Suzan Johnson Cook speaks about turning trials into triumphs, and what she calls destiny decisions. "At some point you have to close the chapter and say, 'Okay, this is the decision I made. I won't make it like that again, but I'm going to move on.' I don't have sleepless nights, because I go to bed in peace, knowing that I've made the best decision that I could make with what I had at hand. I call it becoming a woman of destiny by turning trials into triumphs. Destiny decisions mean you put your own priorities first, rather than allowing others to tell you what's important to you and for you, and ultimately it helps you be a balanced person."

OWN YOUR SUCCESSES

While it's important to own your decisions and their consequences, it is equally important to own the successes.

OWN YOUR DECISIONS, SUCCESSES, FAILURES AND FINANCES

So what is success exactly? Based on the desires we have for our lives, we all define success differently. Some women define success as being able to stay home with the kids while others define it as reaching the C-Suite.

How do you define it? Whatever success means to you, it starts with making up your mind to give it your best shot.

Those who achieve real success understand what that term means to *them*. Those who don't achieve real success are often the ones who allow others to define it for them. In his book *The Successful Mistake* Matthew Turner suggests that success is about who you want to be or what kind of legacy you want to leave behind. It's not about what someone else wants for you. It all comes down to finding meaning in what you are doing.

"IT AIN'T BRAGGING IF YOU DONE IT..."

When you get what you want, and when you do something well, learn how to be your own advocate, your own personal public relations officer. You need to be able to share and promote your successes. Men seem to be able to do this exceptionally well without feeling guilty or worrying that it might look like they're showing off or bragging. They just own it, and we need to learn to do the same thing. How will anyone know what we're capable of unless we tell them?

Here are some myths that Peggy Klaus busts in her book *Brag! The Art of Tooting Your Own Horn Without Blowing It*:

- Myth 1: A job well done speaks for itself.
- Myth 2: Bragging is something you do during performance reviews.
- Myth 3: Humility gets you noticed.
- Myth 4: I don't have to brag; people will do it for me.
- Myth 5: Good girls don't brag.
- Myth 6: Brag is a four-letter word.

Not all self-promotion comes across as being boastful. There are subtle, yet powerful, ways you can promote yourself and acknowledge the efforts of other team members:

- If someone sends you an email, thanking you for a job well done, forward it to your boss with a note that says, "This makes it all worth it."
- Thank your boss for giving you the opportunity to work with your group and to participate in a particularly rewarding project. Highlight the success of the

project and the glowing efforts of your group. By acknowledging your success and the role other people played in it, you are building your brand as a leader.

- Share your success by acknowledging others more publicly. Circulate an email congratulating your team for a job well done. This will call attention to your achievements as well, and, again, will highlight your skills as a leader.
- Learn to say thank you: when given a compliment, accept it graciously. And then stop talking. Avoid phrases like, "I was just lucky." Rather, replace them with, "Thank you. I'm proud of the achievement and grateful for the help I got from my fantastic team."
- In a performance review situation, you can communicate your successes by saying things like, "Thank you for the opportunity to be part of a project where I can use my skill and talent." Or, "I so enjoyed working on project X. I truly appreciated the opportunity to be part of such a great team and to really contribute." These are ways to highlight your success in a way that is not self-serving – and to show your appreciation for the organization that gave you the platform to excel.
- In an interview situation, there is a balance between acknowledging your individual triumphs, and acknowledging what you accomplished as the result of a team. In a team success story, always use the word "we." It shows you're a team player and that you're willing to acknowledge others.
- And always keep in mind the words of professional baseball player Dizzy Dean: "It ain't bragging if you done it!"

But how do you even get to that point where real success is an integral part of your life? Remember that success is not a sprint. We all have to start somewhere, and, according to many successful women, it starts with attitude, passion and hard work. It has nothing to do with the gender myth and everything to do with tenacity, speaking up, keeping relevant, getting uncomfortable, having a good support structure, opening the doors for others, being prepared, being seen and, yes, even being vulnerable. These are the qualities of success, and it all begins with attitude.

OWN YOUR ATTITUDE

Whenever we ask CEOs, executives and directors what they consider to be the most important quality they look for when hiring someone, the unanimous response is flexibility a positive attitude.

"What's going to further your career? There is the expectation that you will deliver results. But, that being said, the next step is having a plan, but a flexible plan, that says, 'I know where I want to go, but I am open to experience and recognize that every experience in the workplace is an opportunity for growth,'" says Arlette Guthrie. And it's a lot easier to have a positive attitude if you love what you do.

It is as simple as that. When you are passionate about something, it is the driving force that pushes you to achieve no matter what the challenge. It's the force that impels you to keep going. Passion gives you meaning; it is the reason you wake up in the morning. It's the reason you persist, and the reason you work hard.

Central to an attitude of success is your fundamental belief that it takes hard work. And hard work takes time. There is no substitute for putting in the time. In the end, it all comes down to hard work and making the necessary sacrifices along the way to achieve your goals and become the best version of yourself.

THE GENDER MYTH

The reality is we still live in a largely male-dominated workforce, but in all our interviews for this book, successful women have said that gender doesn't have to be a defining factor. You are an equal in your own right, and gender doesn't have to hold you back. It is your mindset and how you show up that defines your success.

We don't have to act or behave like men in order to get ahead. Actually, it's quite the opposite. We need to embrace the qualities that distinguish us as women, and use them to our advantage.

TRIPLE YOUR TENACITY AND SPEAK UP!

Tenacity is a key driver that has accelerated many careers. It's about not giving up, regardless of what the obstacles are. It's about telling yourself that you'll keep going, even when you encounter setbacks. It's about facing your fears and taking action despite them.

How can anyone recognize your brilliance when you're hiding it by staying silent? When you don't speak up, you cheat yourself out of the opportunity to promote yourself and your ideas. That can often be challenging in a male-dominated meeting, so plan to make liberal use of logic, preparation and diplomacy to make people aware of what you are saying.

When stating your opinion, always do the research to back it up. If you state your opinion and follow it with a sound rationale, your proposals are much more likely to be considered. Others may not agree with what you are saying, but having justification backed by research makes you more credible.

"It's important to know your craft, and know it really well," says Guthrie. "If you're going to take a position, you need to have some compelling information in order to drive your argument, but also enhance your credibility. It's always been important to me to go the extra mile in terms of research, in terms of connecting, or getting the background information or data necessary to be confident in your position."

VISIBILITY IS CREDIBILITY

What we see time after time, as Sheryl Sandberg famously said, is that "women may take the chairs in the boardroom, but they're not actually 'at the table' and if they are at the table, they're not leaning in. Being visible is a critical part of your career success."

The lesson is *don't* care so much what other people think. To win, you need to participate. If you open yourself up to opportunities, they will always come to y o u . In addition, try to make your mark from the start.

Indeed, you may want to take advice from a prominent Human Resources professional: "Say what you want to say early because if you wait for a year and only then start raising your hand, it might be too late. They might have written you off. Never limit yourself in your thinking."

REINVENTION, RELEVANCE AND RELATABILITY

Change is as natural as breathing, and we need to embrace those changes. We can't get stuck in our old ways. Indeed, if we want to keep moving forward, we need to keep ourselves current. Sometimes we even need to reinvent ourselves, but always, always, with our end goal in mind.

Of course growth can be uncomfortable, but if you are too comfortable, and you are not challenging yourself in any way, you may not be growing. It's easy to get stuck in a comfort zone when you know the job, the situation and the relationship. Challenge yourself. And don't wait until "one day," because that day may never come. Challenging yourself will never feel easy, so you may as well do it today. Tim Ferriss says that success can be measured by the number of uncomfortable conversations you're willing to have.

As you are reading this, think about one thing you have been meaning to do, but haven't because you've been procrastinating. It can be anything from learning a new computer program to finishing your degree. Guess what? Today is a great day to get it started!

As an Editorial Producer for a global network like CNN, Nadia has constantly had to learn about new social media platforms as news-gathering tools. "You have to be able to be nimble," she says. "For example, someone can tweet something about a news event and I have had to track that person down to put them on air. I couldn't do this if I didn't fully understand and embrace social media, which has been a challenge for someone of my generation. I have learned to de-mystify so many things and learned not to be scared of new technology and new platforms. It's been uncomfortable, but I have learned to make the uncomfortable comfortable."

YOUR PERSONAL BOARD OF DIRECTORS

No matter what your goals are and how they relate to your definition of success, ensure you have a good support structure – whether that's family, friends or others you can depend on. These are the people who will push you and support you.

OWN YOUR DECISIONS, SUCCESSES, FAILURES AND FINANCES

In fact, one of the greatest gifts women can give other women is mentorship. This is not only limited to executives and directors. We can all be mentors and it is our responsibility to provide guidance and support to those around us. This is an approach to success in a male-dominated workplace put forward by Gail Evans, author of *She Wins, You Win*, and it is an attitude that will yield far better results than jealousy and revenge. Unfortunately, as Edith Venter has found, that mindset is sadly common. "We sabotage ourselves, and one another too," she says. "I watch women who absolutely pull other successful women down – it's a jealousy thing. We would be so much stronger if we uplifted one another and helped one another along the way, because then it just grows in strength. We are all here for a reason and we need to work together. Don't make people feel threatened; make people feel part of your climb to success."

Jenni Newman also subscribes to the philosophy of mutual support. "I believe there is good in everyone," she says. "I feel that my responsibility is to bring out the good in people and offer help when they need it. It is amazing what one little bit of assistance can do for someone's career, and the kind of confidence it can give a person. I have been very blessed with people who have helped me and, in turn, I feel I have a duty and responsibility to pay it forward. When you have faith in others and you show them that you believe they can reach their goals, it is truly remarkable how often they will rise to the challenge and fulfill your faith in them."

OWN YOUR VULNERABILITY

Vulnerability comes from *vulnus*, the Latin word for "wound." It is "the state of being open to injury, or appearing as if you are." It might be emotional, like admitting that you're in love with someone who might only like you as a friend, or it can be visible, like the vulnerability of a soccer goal that's unprotected by any defensive players. Vulnerability is a concept that is quite daunting at first. However, in her research on the topic of shame and vulnerability, Brené Brown, found that those who embraced vulnerability felt it made them stronger, not weaker.

"Follow your dreams," advises philanthropist and entrepreneur Tracey Webster. "If your dream is to be the president, don't worry about what others think, and don't let the seeds of doubt be sewn in your spirit. Keep focused on the goal and go for it, and remember it takes hundreds of failures along the way to be successful. Share your dreams, rally your cheerleaders around you, live an authentic life, make yourself vulnerable. We don't do this enough – it's a myth that women must be hard and strong in the workplace. Trust comes through showing your vulnerable side because you become human. It allows other people to share when they have a bad day, and you respect each other more. Be vulnerable and encourage others to do the same; you'll be surprised by the outcome."

OWN YOUR FAILURES

Failure is a part of almost everyone's journey. Founders, inventors, athletes, it doesn't matter – everyone's success is built on a previous failure. And, as beauty is in the eye of the beholder, so is failure. Failure should not be viewed as shameful. In fact, failure is one of life's greatest lessons if you choose to see it that way.

Some of the greatest inventions we use today are actually a result of failure. Did you know that bubble wrap was created by accident? It was actually never originally intended for packaging purposes. When engineers Marc Chavannes and Al Fielding created bubble wrap in 1960, it was an attempt to create a trendy new textured wallpaper, and it was a complete disaster. They later attempted to market it as housing insulation. That was a disaster too. But they kept at it. The turning point was when IBM used it as packaging to transport a new computer, and it became a roaring and lucrative success.

Today, few people even realize that bubble wrap began as a total failure. Imagine if Chavannes and Fielding had decided to give up? Sometimes the biggest turning points are just around the corner of failure, and we need to find it within ourselves to push a little bit further if we want to reap the rewards.

Instead, we tend to agonize over our perceived failures. We battle to forgive ourselves and we hold on to our failures, using them as reasons not to move forward on a decision or an action. Failure often becomes the self-fulfilling prophecy that reinforces your determination not to try to accomplish the impossible. And, of course, when we make mistakes, or things don't work out as we'd hoped, it's perfectly natural to go through a period of questioning and regret. But the trick is to give those put-down periods a time limit, and then choose to move on.

We need to push through the fear of failing again, especially after we've been burned. Here are two excellent techniques to help you overcome the fear of failure.

The first technique is EQ expert Daniel Goleman's "rewriting reality." If you're anxious about the outcome of an important presentation, for example, take a moment to imagine a few alternative outcomes, ranging from the presentation going smoothly to it failing completely. List them all. Describe your way of speaking, what the audience looks like, and their reactions to you. Write down every possible scenario you can imagine, good and bad. As the list grows, your anxiety should subside, because now it's not an unknown factor any more. Now you've considered every possible option. Now you're prepared for it.

The second technique for overcoming fear of failure is visualization. Take some quiet time to recreate a vivid mental image of a triumphant moment in your life. Immerse yourself in your feelings of achievement and empowerment at that wonderful moment. Our minds are incredibly powerful, and it is critical that we keep a mental inventory of our past successes. If you haven't built your PEMD yet (Chapter 1), do it now. Write out all the things you have done well, the good decisions you have made, all the times you received praise, all the things that give you a sense of achievement. You need to be able to press the override button when you experience a moment of failure and call your triumphs to mind. Creating a PEMD is an effective way to keep your wins on file so you can pull them up when you are experiencing fear or self-doubt.

When we asked a well-known radio personality what advice she would give her younger self regarding failures, she responded, "I would beg myself, plead with myself, to forgive myself quicker. I really spent too much time crucifying myself for the things I felt I didn't do right, or I felt I could have done better. The only person who remembers is actually you."

Failure can teach us valuable lessons. Even the most successful people fail now and again. There's nothing wrong with making some mistakes along the way, as long as we learn and grow from them one way or another.

So, how do we fix our failures, learn from them and become stronger because of them? Without fear or blame, we look back. As Tracey Webster advises, "be analytical about the past and emotional about the future." We calmly analyze where things went wrong; we look for things that could have been done differently. We research. We ask for advice. And we stack up all that newfound knowledge and the experience that comes with it for next time.

If you're trying something for the first time, expect a period of trial and error. We cannot be experts in everything, and often we have to learn as we go. When you try something and the result is not successful, own it. When you own your story, you take away any power other people have to make you feel inadequate. As Brown writes, this puts you in charge of how the story is written, and the best part is "we get to narrate the ending."

We cannot talk about failure without talking about accountability. You need to be responsible for your thoughts, attitude and actions. If you attempt something and failure is the result, the only way forward is to have an open and honest conversation about why the situation played out as it did. One cannot blame external situations or circumstances. At the end of the day, we are responsible for our own successes and failures. If someone who reports to you makes a massive error, before you blame them remember that you are responsible for their output. Was it your responsibility to check their work? If you don't win a pitch at work, or bring in any new sales, is it really because the clients are just not buying, or because the economy is terrible? Have you honestly asked yourself if you did the necessary preparation for the meeting? Did you put in enough hours making calls this month? Did you have a plan in place?

We may not always be responsible for the situation or the outcome, but we can always be responsible for our reaction to it. Mainly, when you fail, get right back up and get back to work. Don't be discouraged by failure, and never let it stop you from pursuing your dreams. Do you know what failure often means? In many cases it means you're stretching yourself to the limits.

DEVELOPING ROCK-HARD RESILIENCE

Resilience is a key tool in helping you overcome failure. It may not be a trait that comes naturally to everyone, but we can all learn to develop it so that we're better equipped to cope with failure and face it head on.

- Be realistic: Don't zoom in to your failure. View it with a realistic perspective. Will it really matter in a year's time?
- Be grateful: Choose to be grateful– grateful that you had the opportunity to learn; grateful that you're wiser for it, stronger for it and better prepared for the future.
- Believe in yourself: Develop an unconditional belief in your self-worth and maintain your self-confidence both in the good times and the bad.
- Be optimistic: View failure as an experience. Failure doesn't have to be the end; it can be the beginning. In fact, something is only a complete failure if there is absolutely no solution to the problem, and that is very rarely the case.

OWN YOUR FINANCES

We realized it was important to include a section on owning your finances, a key imperative for every woman, but neither of us felt well equipped to provide professional advice in this regard. We called on author and financial planner Sylvia Walker to explain her insights to us. We found her thoughts and advice to be so useful that we have included it in detail in this section on how to truly own your finances:

We expect career success to be associated with financial rewards, but you would be surprised to learn the extent to which many supposedly highly successful women struggle with their finances. In fact, money underpins all our decisions in life, and it is impossible to own our success if we are not in control of our finances. If our money is in disarray, it will directly impact on all other facets of our lives.

Money is a silent force in our lives. It's a means to an end, an inanimate object, yet it drives so many of our decisions. We never seem to have enough of it, and the more we earn, the more we spend. The world we live in is very competitive, and we are often judged by material possessions like homes, cars, furnishings, and fancy holidays. Often, whilst chasing the dream of success, we get caught up in the illusions of success, and end up with spiraling debt, insufficient savings and a tendency to live for today. All of this can leave us financially vulnerable, as we seldom consider the day when the well of money will dry up.

As we travel the road of life, money forms our foundation, impacting on us directly at each stage. We all have aspirations and goals, both for ourselves and our children (if we have them), but there are also unexpected detours that we may face along the way. Being in control and owning your finances means planning for future dreams and goals (as opposed to incurring debt), and ensuring that any detours do not each become a financial crisis. We shouldn't wait for disaster to strike before we start making smart decisions around our money.

Consider some of the curveballs life can throw at us, like divorce, illness, [being fired or laid off], or death of a partner. Some of us end up in a debt trap, others have businesses that go insolvent. All of these situations can cripple one financially if there was no proper planning.

It is also critical to realize that one day our income will dry up. We need to plan for that day and make sure that there will be money for us and our family to continue with our lifestyles. Whether it is illness, disability, retrenchment, death or old age, protecting our income is a vital part of owning our money.

Retirement waits for all of us, and even though the concept of retirement has changed over recent years, having money at 60 or 65 gives us choices, like how we spend our time, as opposed to having to keep working just to survive every month.

For women, retirement can be a particularly harsh experience. After a lifetime of caring and nurturing, many women simply fail to plan adequately for old age, either because they have relied on their partners, or because they simply started saving too late themselves. Because women tend to outlive men by around five years, they should be saving more each month than their male counterparts. This is often not the reality.

Some women are fortunate to have pension or 401K funds at work in addition to Social Security. Preserve that money if you change jobs; it will be very difficult to catch up that lost time in the future. As the average woman lives for 20 or more years after retirement, realize too that Social Security alone will not be sufficient. You will have to have additional savings for retirement. Saving for old age is not a luxury, but a necessity that should be the priority of each and every person.

Owning our money means owning our future. Marital status has little to do with it. Having a husband or partner may bring some form of financial comfort in that the bills are shared, but as a woman, you still need to manage your own money, as your partner should manage his or hers.

"Be proactive and make smart decisions to place yourself in the driving seat of your finances. Start by asking yourself some rather tough questions. *Who is in control of my money? Do I work to enrich my life, and do I have the peace of mind that my future will be certain and exciting? Or do I work just to service debts and pay monthly expenses? Do I have a rather vague view of my financial future?* Depending on your answers, you might want to consider some of these tips:

- Live the life you can afford: Take stock of your situation, be realistic, and live a life that is within your means, not the life you want people to think you can afford. Stop waiting to win the lottery. Realize that the money you have is all you have to work with. Make it work for you.

- Balance your priorities: Avoid living for today at the expense of tomorrow. People often say they do not have money to save. The reality actually lies in how they choose to spend their money. Balancing the wants of today and the needs of tomorrow is key. Understand this, and get this right.

- Plug the holes: Draw up a budget to understand where you are spending your money. You will then be able to make informed decisions about what behavior to change so that you can utilize your money more productively.

- Tackle your debt: Work out how much interest you are paying monthly on your debts. Now multiply that by 12 to see how much this is in a year. Don't forget to include your home loan or car repayments in this calculation. It can be a rather frightening picture. Start eliminating your debts by paying them off one at a time. Cut up your cards if necessary, and, with time and discipline, you will systematically bring your debts down to a more acceptable level. You can then use the money you spent each month on paying your debts to save for future goals.

- Draw up a financial plan: Some people say they will do financial planning when they have enough money. Plan with what you have, and you will end up with enough money. There is no one-size-fits-all approach; rather, consult a professional financial advisor who will draw up a plan for you, and evaluate and adapt that plan annually to make sure you are on track to reaching your goals. Your plan should include a valid will, medical coverage, an emergency fund, income protection (against death, disability and severe illness), as well as investment and retirement planning.

Making changes and taking control may take some time. Do not lose faith or falter. You might have cultivated some bad habits along the way, but stay focused on your end goal. The reward is simple: owning our finances means owning our future, and gives us the perfect platform on which to build success in all other spheres of our lives. We can check that box, and focus our energy on activities and actions that ignite our passions, knowing that financially we will be secure, no matter what happens down the line.

OWN YOUR DECISIONS, SUCCESSES, FAILURES, AND FINANCES...IN A FLASH

- There is no such thing as the perfect decision.
- Listen to your intuition more often. Next time you're making a decision ask yourself, *What would I tell my best friend to do?*
- Once you've made your decision, go for it.
- Weigh the pros and cons, and explore the worst-case scenarios.
- Create your own definition of success.
- Cultivate the qualities of success: be resilient, be passionate, have the right attitude and work hard.
- Become your own personal public relations officer – publicly share and promote your successes.
- Make your future goals the blueprint for your decisions.
- Build your Positive Emotional Memory Database™ to boost your confidence and sense of achievement whenever you need it most.
- Failure is inevitable, but it isn't permanent – it's an opportunity to learn.
- Take control of your finances by living the life you can afford, tackling your debt, and planning for retirement and emergencies.

8 Own
YOUR ASK

Asking for help does not mean that we are weak or incompetent. It usually indicates an advanced level of honesty and intelligence.

- ANNE WILSON SCHAEF

If there's something you want, something you really want, such as a raise, a bigger opportunity, more responsibility, a chance to prove yourself, constructive feedback, or even a little extra help around the house, do you ask for it?

Many of us don't.

Many of us live with self-limiting beliefs or we repeat disempowering stories to ourselves such as, *I don't really deserve to earn that much.* Or, *I can't ask for more money, I'll look greedy.* The most common things that stop us from asking for what we want are insecurity and fear: fear of appearing weak, of appearing arrogant or entitled, of being humiliated, of being rejected, and fear of hearing the word "no."

But have you ever wondered what would happen if you *did* ask? Imagine getting a positive response to your request. What would it be like to secure that raise or promotion? Wouldn't you feel validated and rewarded for all of the work and effort you have made?

We need to start trusting ourselves more and build the confidence and sense of self-worth to ask for what we want. If you could ask for anything you wanted, what would it be? What is stopping you from asking? What have you not asked for in the past that you now regret? How might your life be different if you had asked? Conversely, what have you asked for and received?

Too many opportunities are lost because someone didn't have the courage to ask for what they wanted. Too often, women in the corporate world feel they are not being appreciated or being given the opportunity to reach their highest potential, but most of us don't really ask for it. Typically, men are not afraid to tell their bosses what they're great at – and then they back up their assertions with numbers. Typically, women don't. But unless you tell your boss about the great thing you've done, they'll likely never realize it. If you don't raise your voice to change the situation, why would they ever offer it to you? Silence reflects acceptance.

Therefore, if you want to change your situation, you need to change your actions and change your assumptions.

NEVER ASSUME THAT SOMEONE ELSE KNOWS WHAT YOU WANT

Do you ever find yourself thinking, *They must recognize the great work I am doing; I'm sure they will reward me for it*? Sadly, this is rarely the case. If you want to be noticed, take our advice from Chapter 7 and be your own advocate. If you want more, you have to learn to ask for it.

This holds true for your personal life as much as your professional one. If you're unhappy about something, you need to speak up in order to change it. If you don't communicate and ask for what you want, you can't expect others to guess what's going on.

For months, a young mother harbored a grudge against her husband for not helping enough with the kids. But when we asked her if she'd brought this up with her husband, she said no. She felt it was obvious that she was tired and needed a little more help. We explained to her that he probably had no idea that she felt so tired; he probably assumed she had it all under control. She took our advice and asked him for some help. Not only did he happily agree to help a lot more, he loved playing a larger role in caring for the kids.

So ask. By being willing to ask, you could get a promotion, an upgrade, a more flexible work schedule, a discount, time off, or help with the housework. After all, what's the worst that could happen? The person could say no. So what? You're not any worse off for having asked. And if you get a no, the ask is still not wasted: the simple act of asking presents the opportunity to understand what is preventing you from getting a yes.

"Let people know where you want to go," advises Nima Ahmed, the Director of Programming at CNN. "We often feel like we need people to come to us, but you'd be surprised when you let people know what your goals are, by the number of people who will help you."

You'll never be successful at asking for something substantial if you don't inherently believe that you deserve it. Know that you deserve it. If you need to, go back to Chapter 1 and revisit Owning Your Headspace. Have the confidence and self-belief to go after what you want. Believe in yourself. Believe that it's possible and go in asking for it like it is already yours. Your body language will reflect your level of confidence, so go in with a smile, your shoulders back and your head held high. This will assist you in coming across with the necessary confidence and competence – and the people around you will sense it. Conversely, if you doubt yourself, others will pick up on that and, in turn, they'll start to have doubts as well. Visualize yourself asking for what you desire and receiving a yes. Imagine how it will feel. This will put you in the right mindset so you can approach the conversation with a sense of self-assurance.

The future doesn't belong to those who sit back wishing and hoping that their lives will somehow become better without changing their behavior. The future belongs to those people who step up. It be- longs to those who ask.

So, go ahead. Ask for what you want.

THE HOW OF YOUR ASK

The first step is making the decision and giving yourself permission to ask. The second step is crafting a way of asking that feels comfortable for you. We call this the HOW of your ask.

Before you begin to build your ask, do the necessary research to ensure what you are asking for is a realistic possibility. You can't ask for something that is completely unreasonable or unrealistic, like asking for remote working arrangements when company policy strictly prohibits it, or asking for an increase that well exceeds your market-related salary. We are not discouraging you from asking, but we are encouraging you to make sure that your asks are well-researched, well thought-out and persuasively substantiated.

ASK WITH THE RIGHT ATTITUDE

Women are sometimes afraid to ask for what they want and need because they don't value themselves. "Man don't have problems asking for promotions or raises," says Ahmed. "But, maybe because of our upbringing, we aren't as likely to do this. We don't say anything until we're approached." You may wait forever, and you should never underestimate your worth to an organization. Build a strong case for why you deserve what you are asking for and share the evidence that you have researched to substantiate your argument. Don't be afraid to challenge and argue your case.

We do need to learn to ditch the guilt when it comes to asking. As women, many of us have been socialized to be conciliatory and undemanding, which can make us fearful that if we ask for something, we may come across as aggressive and greedy.

One of our clients had a customer who owed her money for services rendered. When Lori asked her whether she had approached this person, our client's response was, "I feel so bad about asking her for the money." That's nonsense! The simple fact was that she had done the work – and had even spent some of her own money in order to provide the service. Logically, it makes no sense to feel guilty or apologetic about asking for money owed, yet we often feel this way. If you're ever in a similar situation, remember two golden rules: silence is seen as acceptance, and she who asks first gets what she wants. In a case like this, if this woman couldn't pay out all her creditors, the ones who made the most noise would get paid first.

It can often be a jolt to adjust to the rough and tumble of a corporate environment, where assertiveness is valued. Women who grew up in an environment where a woman's role was to cook, look after the kids and be politely submissive often have to make a difficult adjustment. "I realized that to survive I had to wake up," one of our colleagues recalls. "I had to be myself, and not fear anyone."

Sometimes, even when we have the confidence, when we assert ourselves, when we ask *the ask* we still get a no. But bear in mind that just because someone says no to your current request, doesn't mean that there isn't a yes in the future with a change of circumstances. In general, when a woman hears a decision being given as no, she hears, "It's never going to happen." In order to overcome our fear of rejection, we need to remember that a decision given as no can sometimes mean "not right now." "No" is not a personal attack. It could simply be a matter of circumstances. For example, the company might be under financial strain and not able to meet your request at the time.

EARN YOUR ASK

Don't talk about how hard you're working because it doesn't help. You get paid for output, not input. When asking for anything related to a promotion or increase, you must quantify the value you add and focus on your positive impact on the business.

Do you want a promotion? Getting one can be very much in your control. You promote yourself every time you take on a new responsibility. One of the most important ways to come out ahead is continually *asking* for more responsibility. Volunteer for additional assignments. Ask your boss what you have to do to qualify for an increase. Most people do only what is asked of them, but in *The Law of Success*, Napoleon Hill says we need to do more than we are being paid for. This is what will elevate you above your colleagues, so make it your job to keep asking for more. And whenever you are given a new responsibility, do it quickly and do it well.

Fewer things are more important in helping you getting paid what you are really worth than your reputation for speed and dependability. Be the kind of person your boss can count on to get a job done quickly and well. Treat every assignment you receive as if it is a test upon which your future career depends. You'll eventually rise to the level of responsibility you are willing to accept.

When that time comes, build your case like a lawyer would and then approach your boss. Most people simply say that they need more money, but you need a different strategy. Take the emotion out of it. Be logical. Be factual. Put together a list of the jobs that you're now actively taking on, how many years you've been with the company, what the market-related salary is and what your qualifications are. List the additional experience you've gained and all the new skills you've developed. Show the financial impact of your work, the value you add to the bottom line and make your contribution to the company clear.

PRACTICE YOUR ASK

Rehearsals are not only for actors. Grab a good friend who values you and understands you, and go over the conversation a few times, especially if a conversation like this doesn't come naturally to you.

Julia Lazarus emphasizes the importance of practicing these crucial conversations. "Talk it through with a trusted friend or two. Discuss what you want, why you think you deserve it and what objections you might face. I've found that having a personal 'Board of Directors' – successful people who are invested in you – is a great approach." Lazarus practices what she preaches and says that, as a result, she achieves her goals. "I asked my company to give me an expatriate assignment and to sponsor my Executive MBA. They did both."

Dr. Colinda Linde, a clinical psychologist, advises preparing by saying that number out loud before you go in. Look in the mirror and say, "I am worth X." It may feel silly at first, but you can't risk saying the number for the first time in that meeting. You need to own it in your mind first. So prepare, practice and repeat. Go in and do it. If you have done your homework, you will feel safer and far more comfortable.

CULTIVATE YOUR OWN BOARD OF ADVISORS

If you really don't know where to begin, ask someone who's already done it before you. Look around – there are so many people who have achieved exactly what you want. Instead of reinventing the wheel, ask them for their advice. Don't demand their help; acknowledge their talents and experience, and let them know why you're specifically coming to them for help. Make them feel appreciated first. Then, invite them for a cup of coffee or, if you work with them, offer to bring some coffee to their desk for a quick chat.

Melissa Dawn Simkins calls the people she seeks guidance and advice from her "brand squad." When executives, athletes and influential leaders want to know how to build a brand of global influence, they call Simkins. She is the authority on champion brand leadership and her creative influence is the brains behind some of the world's most beloved brands, such as Kraft and P&G. "It doesn't need to be all women, and not everyone on your brand squad has to be someone who can support your career," she says. "My brand squad has included a male friend who made sure I took breaks from work to have fun and a woman who gave me relationship advice. Having this kind of network will keep you from becoming one-dimensional."

You'll be surprised at how willing people are to share their own experiences and advice with you, as long as you acknowledge and honor them. When it came to approaching our interviewees for this book, we were delighted by how open and willing these amazing women were to share their journeys. Don't assume people are too busy for you or wouldn't be interested in helping you. Just ask. You'll be astounded at what you can learn.

TIME YOUR ASK

According to Linde, there is research that suggests the best times for an ask are specifically Tuesday, Wednesday, and Thursday at 11 am. On Mondays, people are still easing into the week, and on Fridays they are moving towards party mode. And why 11 am? "It's when you are almost at lunch," she says. "You are over the worst part of the day." In addition to choosing your time of day, you also need to look at context.

What's the workload of the person you are asking? Never ask something of someone who isn't happy – if you can see that they are stressed or in a terrible mood, avoid asking until they are more settled. Plan the conversation for a time when your boss is likely to be receptive. So much of what you can get financially and otherwise depends on how the other person feels in the moment – it can be the difference between getting an outright yes or a horrific no.

If you are asking for time off, ask earlier than you need to. If you ask a few months prior, your boss is more likely to agree to your request, because you're probably the only person who's thinking ahead. If you ask two weeks beforehand, especially if you're asking to take time off over a public holiday when several other people have already requested it, you might not get the answer you are hoping for. Your boss will also be in a better headspace when not snowed under by an avalanche of last-minute requests.

BE GRACIOUS

There is a difference between confidence and arrogance. Sure, you have every right to ask, but make sure the manner in which you do it evokes an open response. Always maintain a professional demeanor, be polite, say please and thank you, and take care not to appear entitled.

There are ways you should ask and ways you shouldn't. When you're ready to ask for an increase, arm yourself with all the right tools. And don't commit these cardinal errors:

- Don't use someone else's salary as the basis for the discussion
- Don't talk about how great you are and how useless everyone else is
- Don't go over your direct manager's head without discussing it with them first
- Don't send an email on the subject of remuneration copying other people.

Instead, Human Resources professionals say we should ask with a combination of "humility, conviction and determination."

When asking for something like a promotion or salary increase, know how to ask and then stop talking. It's up to the other person to accept, reject, counter or negotiate.

People receive requests for help and support differently. The person could feel like a boundary has been crossed if what you're asking for seems like too much. While you don't want to hold yourself back from asking for what you really want, be sure to give others a chance to offer what they feel comfortable with. In all likelihood, they'll offer you more if you do them that courtesy.

When someone says to Nadia, "You work at CNN, and I really want a job there. Can you get me an interview?" She usually refers them to the online job board. But if someone says, "I'd love the chance to work at CNN. Do you have any advice for me?" she feels much more inclined to go out of her way to help, because she feels like her boundaries have been respected. This approach comes across as far less demanding and entitled.

BE SPECIFIC

Be clear about what you want. Nobody's going to be able to help you until you are specific about what you are trying to achieve. Whenever Lori meets with her mentor, she emails him her objectives before the session so he can prepare, and she can get the most out of it.

When you're clear about what you want, you can focus on the specifics. If you want more money or more responsibility, be prepared to substantiate why you deserve what you are asking for and be specific about exactly how much you want. This is especially important when it comes to pay raises, bonuses, advancement opportunities, and requesting more responsibility.

For most of us, asking for a bigger salary is unnatural and uncomfortable. Most of us have no idea how to walk in, ask for the money and come out smiling. Do we demand it? Threaten to leave if we don't get it? Plead poverty? Or, do we ignore the situation entirely and trust that the money will somehow magically come to us?

Very often if you want an increase, you have to ask for it. You can't be afraid to say this is what I need and this is what I want. People want to see drive and initiative. And you need to believe you're worth it.

DOUBLE YOUR ASK

Successful people often ask again and again until they get what they want. Did you know that *Harry Potter and the Philosopher's Stone* was rejected by 12 publishers? J.K. Rowling is now one of the richest people in England, with a net worth near $1 billion, because she was tenacious; she kept asking, and she never gave up.

Nikki Cockcroft, who heads the online retailing group of a large retailer, shared her boldest moment with us and it epitomizes tenaciousness to the nth degree: "I met a CEO on a plane when I was still studying, and he said, 'One day when you start working, I would love for you to come work for me.' So three months before I graduated, I went there and he said, 'We can't afford you. We literally cannot pay you anything, and we do not have space for you.' But, I went back every single day for three months until they hired me. And that was the start of my career. I did work for free at the beginning, but I didn't take no for an answer. I knew that I had value to add. And, ironically, those three directors I was dealing with then are still my mentors today."

KNOW YOUR PLANS B, C AND D

If your request for an increase is turned down, ask what exactly you can do to get the increase you want at a later time, and ask when that increase will be payable. Be specific. Be clear. If you get the increase, but it's less than you requested, ask what you need to do to get the rest of your asking salary. Alternatively, if they cannot offer you the full amount immediately, request in writing that the matter is reassessed in six months' time.

Many of us, especially working moms, admit that we would be satisfied with additional flexibility. If your request for more money is not granted, then know exactly what it is that will make you happy if money is not an option for the company. Your plan B could be: "If the increase is not viable at this point, how about I work four days per week?"

DEVELOP A STYLISH ASK

So we have covered the basics on "the ask." You've done the work; you know that you deserve it, you've got a clear vision of what you want and you've got the facts to back it up. You've even got the timing right. Now it's time to actually open your mouth and say the words.

Are you suddenly tongue-tied or brimming with just a little too much force? There are ways to go about asking that are more likely to deliver your desired result. According to Linde, there are three distinct asking styles we typically use when faced with challenging conversations or discussions. Do you recognize yourself in any of them?

PASSIVE: THE SCENIC ROUTE

This is a passive, roundabout way to get to what we are actually asking for. If we're not feeling validated about asking for something, we tend to make ourselves submissive. For example, we start the conversation with an apology by saying something like, "I know you're really busy, and I'm sorry to disturb you, but..." or, "Do you mind? I don't want to inconvenience you..."

There isn't great success in this asking style because appearing timid and insecure (quite likely emphasized by matching body language, such as folded arms and crossed legs) doesn't really inspire a positive impression in the person who's supposed to grant your request.

If your boss asked to reschedule an important meeting with you for the second time, taking the scenic route would look a little like this. First, you'd wait a long time before responding, maybe even up to a month, and when you do finally approach your boss, it's with an apology: "I'm sorry to worry you, but do you mind if we put some time on the calendar? You cancelled about a month ago...but I'm sure you are very busy." You're ultimately diminishing yourself and allowing someone else to take advantage of you.

AGGRESSIVE: I WIN YOU LOSE

This is typically when you demand instead of ask, or you don't express your views on a situation and instead allow your frustration to build until it culminates in an explosion. You are then out of control. The conversation has gone beyond direct and is now abusive. You don't respect the other person's rights and you behave badly. If it's a superior you're interacting with, they may call you in about your behavior and your neglect to follow through on the topic you wanted to discuss. This will likely leave you feeling disempowered. Clearly, there is significant potential for this approach to backfire.

If your boss asked to reschedule an important meeting with you for the second time, taking an aggressive stance would look a little like this: "You are rescheduling again! You are jerking me around. It's enough, now! You are a terrible leader!" This is not a constructive approach and it's definitely not recommended.

ASSERTIVE: IT'S JUST ABOUT THE FACTS

A direct asking style is an assertive asking style. You know what you want and you are able to ask in a way that is polite but candid, and focused solely on the facts. There is little emotion involved. It is very matter-of-fact. The body language here is a relaxed, confident stance, with good eye contact and a moderated voice tone.

If your boss asked to reschedule an important meeting with you for the second time, taking the direct approach would look a little like this: You take immediate action and stick to the facts, saying, "This is the second time we need to reschedule, and I really need this to be a priority, as it affects both of us. Let's find time on our calendars that will work for both you and me."

This is the recommended way to ask. You want to be assertive but you don't want to be aggressive. The aggressive person will demand. The assertive person will ask firmly. Assertive people are friendly and self-assured; they make eye contact and listen to others. They check on the prevailing mood before engaging in the conversation, and they contain their reactions until it is an appropriate time to express their views.

THE EMPATHETIC ASK

Dr. Linde says that assertiveness has one key rule: respect for the opinions of others. This is where empathy comes in. It is about really putting yourself in someone else's place and seeing the scenario from their point of view. For example, if you know someone has not done a task to the standards you would like or their work has slipped and you need to address this, stop to think first if there is a reason for this behavior change. Perhaps they have had a family crisis or a personal problem. Once you have a better understanding of their situation, you can handle it in a calmer and more mindful manner.

If you really cannot find a way forward, then the next step is to recruit a third party to assist and mediate.

If you want to ensure a successful conversation, it might be useful for you to rehearse it ahead of time. This is something Lori subscribes to. She often practices the conversation out loud, as she believes that hearing it aloud helps her structure her thoughts and also get a sense of how the conversation might sound to others. Perhaps it needs to be finessed to be gentler, or perhaps it needs to be more assertive.

ASKING FOR FEEDBACK

When we think about the act of asking in a corporate context, our minds tend to zip straight to salary increases, bonuses and promotions. But what about asking for feedback? We don't see our blind spots; we're not perfect and there is always room for growth. So we need to be brave enough to ask those around us for their input on what we are doing that works and what we are doing that doesn't serve us best.

Don't be shy. Ask for feedback from your bosses, colleagues and friends. Ask how you can do better. Ask if you need to change your approach. Ask *how* you can change your approach. Jack Canfield says that if you take any advice at all from his books, it should be his insights on asking for advice. His approach is to ask, "On a scale of one to ten, how would you rate the meeting we just had? Or me as a manager? Me as a parent? Me as a teacher? This meal? My cooking? This deal? This book?" Any answer less than a ten gets this follow-up question: "What would it take to make it a ten?"

Canfield feels that knowing someone is discontented is not enough; you need to understand exactly where you can improve in order to satisfy them, which creates powerful feedback.

So, request and receive feedback – whether or not you like what you hear. It can be a little distressing to hear opinions that don't correspond with how you view yourself, but it's not going to work if you ask for an opinion and then lay out all the reasons you feel the other person is wrong. Remember that these people are not trying to hurt you; they're trying to help you. When you get feedback, stay neutral. Treat every piece of advice as a gift and say thank you. Be humble and be willing to learn.

Another golden rule of feedback is to avoid one short and very dangerous word. Dr. Linde strongly believes that in *any* crucial conversation, we need to avoid the word "you." When we become angry, it's easy to accuse. "You are being unfair! You promised me. You are being unethical. You are not listening!" As soon as that "you" creeps in, we've crossed the line into aggression. Save the "you" for compliments.

RESPONDING TO AN ASK

If you are on the other side of an ask, always remember that it has often taken the other person immense courage to approach you, so validate and honor the asker even if you cannot accommodate their request. Always be aware of the tone and words you use during your response. Saying no to someone doesn't have to destroy their confidence and self-esteem.

For many of us, giving feedback can actually feel more uncomfortable than receiving it – especially when we need to give feedback to someone who has let us down. In situations where someone hasn't performed their task very well, they probably already know they've disappointed us, so we need to be careful not to do anything to break them down further. A key factor in providing feedback to others is to deal with the task, not the person. Once we make it personal, we create barriers to receptiveness.

The way to handle the situation is to provide constructive feedback on how it *should* have been handled. It's important to remember to avoid the words "but" and "however." These words negate everything you have said before. If you say something like, "I know you tried your best on this proposal but..." whatever comes next has negated anything prior to that. Rather, outline the situation, the task at hand and the suggested approach. For example, you could say, "I know you tried to approach it in this way. If it were me, I would have done X." Or, "I find that when I have to contact a client about money, I will take the following approach ... What really has worked well for me in the past is X...Have you ever tried this?"

When you take the focus away from the individual and place it on yourself, you're sharing your experience and empowering that person to try a new route, without making them feel like they've failed. For example, Nadia does a lot of training for Home Depot and they don't refer to mistakes as failures, but rather "areas of opportunity." By taking a different approach to feedback, it reframes how you view the situation and others will likely be more open to responding to your suggestions in a positive manner.

When approaching these kinds of conversations, you need to be clear about your intent at the outset. What is your purpose in having the conversation? What do you hope to accomplish? What would be an ideal outcome? How do you want the other person to feel afterwards? Once you have answered these questions, make sure your body language reflects this – be open and confident, but not overpowering. Also think about your attitude. Once you know your intention, have an open and positive attitude and believe that the conversation will have a positive outcome.

In order for someone to be open to receiving feedback, they need to feel safe – not like they're being pushed into a corner. When you create that environment of safety, you can talk about anything without the danger of the other person feeling like they're being attacked. Once we start feeling like we're being unfairly criticized, most of us tend to freeze up and our emotions start to take over. The body can't tell the difference between a heated discussion and true danger, so it enters fight-or-flight mode, often at the expense of clear, rational thinking.

In their book *Crucial Conversations*, Kerry Patterson, Joseph Grenny, Ron McMillan, and Al Switzler explain that a safe atmosphere hinges on two key conditions: a feeling of mutual respect, and a common purpose. You can often accomplish both these things by making sure that the people you're in conversation with know their opinions matter. Allow them the opportunity to be listened to and let them know you have heard them. You don't have to agree with them, but it's important to be open to hearing their viewpoints.

In our workshops, we divide feedback into two categories: reinforcing and redirecting. Reinforcing is where positive action needs to be acknowledged and repeated, and redirecting is where alternative action is required. We use the STAR Feedback method: Situation or Task, Action, Result. If someone has done something well, we could say, "You generated X amount of income [situation or task] by being proactive [action], therefore we have increased profitability [result] and you will get a raise."

When we redirect, we give positive actions and results as an alternative to the negative action and the result taken using the STAR model. In this case we could say, "On Thursday, one of our CNN guests didn't make the interview [**situation or task**]. You sent them to the wrong studio [**action**] and because of that, they were late [**result**]. Going forward, please triple-check locations [**alternative action**]. That way, they will make it on air [**alternative result**]."

The key for both reinforcement and redirection is that you are as specific as possible. Just telling someone they have done a great job doesn't let them know exactly what they have done so they can repeat it. The same applies to redirection: letting the person know what alternative action would have had a more positive outcome helps them to take better action in the future. It may also be useful to ask the individual what they could do differently in the future, as opposed to telling them. That way, you engage them actively in the process.

Another way to create a safe space is to allow someone the opportunity to reply the next day or to sleep on it. Have the conversation and then say, "Think about how you would like to approach it and let's touch base tomorrow to finalize the way forward."

Be as good at giving feedback as you are at receiving it, and you'll find that it builds confidence and provides clear direction for you and everybody else on the journey.

OWN YOUR ASK ... IN A FLASH

- Make a list of all the things you would like to ask for but haven't. What are you missing out on because you haven't asked? What would you gain by asking?
- Ask. What's the worst that could happen?
- Keep asking if you don't get the answer you are hoping for. Don't give up.
- Be specific about what you want.
- Ask at the right time: Tuesdays, Wednesdays and Thursdays at 11 am are good times. And ask when your boss is in a receptive mood.
- Don't wait to be given more responsibility; ask for it.
- Don't be passive or aggressive. Focus on a direct asking style and respect the opinions of others.
- Keep emotion out of it. Be prepared and stick to the facts.
- When asking for a salary increase, build a case and show the value you add to the company's bottom line.

- Believe you're worth it.
- Don't let yourself get comfortable. Ask for feedback. Treat every piece of advice as a gift and be willing to learn.
- When you give feedback to others, deal with the task, not the person.

9 Own
YOUR PODIUM

There are always three speeches, for every one you actually gave. The one you practiced, the one you gave, and the one you wish you gave.

– DALE CARNEGIE

Presentations can be written invitations to your success. They shouldn't be avoided; they should be taken full advantage of. Yet many people (you may or may not be one of them) avoid these opportunities at all costs. If you are one of the avoiders, be comforted – you are not alone. Speaking in public is a universal fear. But think about it: When you're asked to give a presentation, you've actually been handed a captive audience, a group of people ready to pay attention to you, ready to listen to your ideas, primed for you to show them how smart, talented, articulate, and capable you are. So why does something that can be so positive cause us so much stress?

Ah. Yes. It's that uncomfortable feeling of having the spotlight turned directly onto *you*. You're not alone if the mere thought of public speaking gets your heart pounding furiously. In workshops from Durban to Dubai, many of our participants admit that they struggle with the fear of speaking in public. Jerry Seinfeld once quipped in a stand-up routine, "According to most studies, people's number one fear is public speaking. Number two is death. Death is number two. Does that sound right? This means to the average person, if you go to a funeral, you're better off in the casket than doing the eulogy."

But, there's no question that your ability to articulate and present yourself with clarity, confidence and charisma in a public arena is critical to your career advancement. Often, the ability to win new clients, get promoted and gain additional exposure is based on how you present yourself publicly. Many leaders attribute their success to their ability to articulate their messages and express their points of view effectively to a group. Recruiters also pay attention to your presentation skills – in some cases they even go to the extent of hiring trained evaluators to assess a candidate's public speaking and ability to communicate.

Presentations are one of your most important opportunities to make an impression, to stand out and enhance your personal brand. It's not simply another boring meeting. Get over thinking of presentations as burdens. Think of meetings and presentations as opportunities. Just by thinking about them differently, you can shift your level of confidence, and that, as you know, is the first step to improving the overall way you are perceived.

As discussed in Chapters 1 and 5, we also need to get over the notion that we have to be perfect in order to step into the spotlight. "I'm afraid of making a fool of myself," you may say. "I'm afraid that I'll forget what I wanted to say, or that I won't be able to hold the audience's attention." But here's the thing: Nobody's expecting us to be utterly flawless. It is impossible. What is possible is constant improvement. What is possible is communicating a little more effectively each time. We can learn how to create stronger connections with our audience, to be more engaging, to tell a more powerful story. But, we have to get out there and do it, and we have to prepare.

Preparation is one of the most powerful tools in both eliminating nerves and connecting with the audience. When you're mentally prepared, it gives you an incredible level of confidence because you have already anticipated and overcome any anxiety. When you're physically prepared, it allows you to own your space, both in terms of how you present yourself upon entering the room and how you conduct yourself during that presentation. If you carefully prepare your content, you can work on being brief and concise, rather than flowery and verbose. You also avoid the potential disaster of what can happen if you try to speak "off the cuff"!

There are many simple strategies and techniques you can use to become an impressive communicator and a more relaxed public speaker. If you're not a natural at this, you can still learn to overcome your fears, and you can develop the skills to deliver more compelling content and present yourself with more charm, confidence and authority.

We both speak regularly in front of small and large audiences, and whenever we share the key components of effective, powerful and career-enhancing presentations in our workshops, people often come back to us later to tell us they're more comfortable and capable than ever when it comes to giving presentations.

The reality is that whether you're giving a presentation in front of a large audience or simply interacting with your manager, knowing how to own your podium is an important skill to hone.

GET THEM HOOKED AND REEL THEM IN

People get up front and speak every day: in meetings, on stages, in front of cameras. Some of them lose us entirely, but some of them hook us and pull us right in, keeping us mesmerized until the very end.

How do they do it?

They have learned how to be H-E-A-R-D:

- H – Hook your audience
- E – Evidence: get the facts
- A – Anecdotes: tell stories
- R – Reel in: recap and relate
- D – Delivery skills: the power of how

OWN YOUR HOOK

Never start your presentation with, "I'm here today to talk about..." Don't do it. It's a total snoozer!

How *do* you start? If you want the most effective hook, if you want to engage your audience immediately, you need to know exactly who that audience is. Once you understand your audience, you can tailor and pitch the talk especially for them.

A strong hook will grab your audience within the first few seconds and will give you an immediate advantage every time you give a presentation. Your hook could be a question, a compelling statement or a fascinating fact. It's the start of a presentation that will change your audience's thoughts, feelings or actions. That's what your presentation must do...ultimately, it needs to affect people.

So, take the time to craft your hook carefully. Ask yourself what you want your audience thinking, feeling and doing (TFD). Once you can answer that, you're in a much stronger position to create a powerful hook. And get creative. If you're going to start with a question, make it a question that your audience will immediately relate to – and a question that your presentation will answer.

Let's say you need to persuade your store associates to sell additional accessories for an item. You could kick off with a question followed by a brief story or anecdote: "Have you ever bought supplies for a home improvement painting project, and when you got home you realized you had forgotten to buy the plastic cloths to protect the furniture? That happened to me last week. It was so frustrating. Well, that is exactly how our customers feel when we forget to recommend all the incidentals they need with their purchase." Now, suddenly, selling accessories is not another vague concept. You need to make things real and relevant to your audience.

We once gave a presentation to a group of pupils in senior primary school to encourage them to become more sensitive to people less fortunate than themselves. We needed a strong hook; we needed to make it real for them. So we asked, "What did you think about on your way to school today? How many of you thought about homework, school lunch or a party on the weekend?" Then we added, "That's what life *should* be like, right? But it isn't so for Jamimah, a girl your age who lives in Southern Africa. Jamimah takes care of her three younger brothers because both of her parents, and her aunts and uncles, have died of HIV/AIDS. Today we will look at what a problem HIV/AIDS is throughout the world; how to appreciate what you have and what we can do to make her life a little easier." It was our way to kick off a heavy subject by making it relevant to a young audience, and the group was enthralled.

By tuning into WIIFM, you're making your presentation relevant to your listeners because the 'me' in this situation is your audience. It's not selfishness; it's human nature. They're wondering, *What's in this for me?* and, *Why should I watch/listen?* Show that you're aware of their needs and desires, remind them of the benefit or value you're going to provide and give it to them early. You need to answer the most important audience question at the beginning of every presentation, and to do it in a way that grabs their attention.

Since everyone is tuned in to WIIFM, if you aren't broadcasting on their station, they won't hear a word you say. They'll also tune out very quickly if you come across as self-indulgent. You need to be inclusive when sharing your message, so avoid using the word "I" and include more "you" and "we." You don't want to kick off with something bland, self-focused and obvious, such as, "The reason I am presenting this today is to persuade you to buy this software package because I know how much it will increase sales." Rather, pose an interesting question involving a number, such as, "Did you know that switching to automated sales software can increase your revenue by as much as 75%?"

When you want people to agree with you, it is vital to accentuate the positives first – and using numbers, especially specific amounts or percentages, always adds power to your statements.

OWN YOUR STORY

When you need to convince your audience that they should believe in your idea as much as you do, you need to find the most compelling evidence to support your message, and you need to make sure that your content is 100% accurate. If it's not, you will lose credibility before you even start. Your evidence can come in the form of data, facts or statistics. If you want to persuade your audience to be more conscious of multi-platform marketing, you need to give them examples of the top companies that are doing it most effectively or give them statistics of the increased numbers of customers connected to these marketing platforms. You can also disprove common misconceptions, provide thought-provoking numbers, or post a number and ask the audience to guess what it represents relative to your topic. The greatest secret behind any memorable presentation, and the one technique that really gives you the edge, is the ability to tell fantastic anecdotes that make a point related to the topic and help the audience learn something new.

It's interesting to note that while people have no problem sharing personal stories in coffee talk or casual conversations, they often forget to include them as powerful tools of persuasion in their presentations. In many cases, the most memorable and impactful stories have an edge (such as humor, emotion or inspiration) that provides a fresh perspective on the topic. Nadia often tells the story of a friend who ruined her new car by pumping it full of diesel instead of regular gasoline. New to America, she didn't stop to ask for help and somehow physically forced the unfamiliar nozzle into the gas tank, causing thousands of dollars' worth of damage to her car. It's a humorous cautionary tale that lends itself very neatly to highlighting the potentially negative consequences of going it alone, and emphasizing the importance of being willing to ask for assistance.

If you are the final speaker, leave room in your speech to include anecdotes about things that have been said and done in the room during the course of the event. It's an effective tool for keeping the content of what you're saying relevant to your audience and a way of showing your interest in the people you're talking to. Humor is always a good strategy to make your audience feel warm and connected, but be careful to avoid insults and keep things lighthearted.

REEL IN: RECAP AND RELATE

Now is the time to finish with the same level of confidence that you started with. The way you end is as important as the way you begin. Keep in mind what you wanted people thinking, feeling and doing (TFD) as you close your presentation, bringing in your evidence and anecdotes to move your point forward and drive the message home. Like hooking a fish, this is your final chance to land your audience before you lose the floor and they slip away.

If possible, don't hold a Q&A at the very end of your presentation; it saps the audience's energy. If you do want to facilitate a Q&A, schedule it as the second-to-last item of your presentation and time it carefully so that you can still end with that all-important reel-in that is ultimately intended to deliver on what you promised and achieve the purpose of your presentation.

Recap your key points. Recommend steps of action. Remind your audience what the benefits to them will be if they take your advice. The very best finish is a call to action that gives the audience something specific to do next. Give your audience something concrete to do, like "send me an email, sign up for the training and newsletter, or approve the budget." Stick to your theme and keep asking yourself, *What do I want my audience thinking, feeling and doing)?*

Here's how Kat Cole, CEO of Focus Brands, connected with her audience of industry peers by focusing on what she wanted them TFD from start to finish. It was a presentation on the importance of human resources in leading an organization, and Cole had initially planned to detail specific ways human resources leaders could improve the talent in their organizations. But after talking to members of the audience, she found out what was really on their minds: the economy, the constant changes in their companies, the mergers and acquisitions, bankruptcies, and changes in ownership. Cole recognized that her audience desired a different version of her message. Instead of providing the technical content she'd prepared, she realized what she really wanted the audience thinking, feeling and doing was related to how they could be more comfortable and confident in their roles leading their organizations and in their ability to survive all these changes.

Her revised focus made her presentation far more relevant and effective. She made an immediate connection with her audience by asking, "By a show of hands, how many of you in this room are going through a merger, an acquisition, a bankruptcy, or a change in ownership?" There were very few people without their hands raised. She built on that connection and the presentation was a big success. She ended her presentation even more powerfully with this reel-in: "You are not alone in the changes you are going through. Go back to your employees, your peers and your organization's leadership, and share what you've learned today. Position yourself as a leader who has the confidence and the capability to take on greater responsibility and continue to move up as your organization evolves."

She tuned in to what the audience needed and successfully incorporated that into her message because she was very clear on what she wanted them thinking, feeling and doing all the way through.

DELIVERY SKILLS: THE POWER OF HOW

With your powerful hook and reel all set and ready to launch, the next step is to execute your presentation with stellar delivery skills. How you deliver your speech is as important as your content.

And that means you've got to prepare, prepare, prepare.

Preparation is extremely important. You have to build in the time to do it properly. Before you give your presentation, bounce it off of a few people. Most likely, they'll each have a different perspective and different questions. If it is at a board meeting, talk to representatives of the various heads of department who will be attending to get different points of view, because what you might think is the answer to everything probably has a few nuances or risks that you need to overcome.

As we discussed in Chapter 2, first impressions are everything. Before going into a presentation, you need to decide how you want your audience to perceive you and dress the part. You need to understand your audience and be aware that different audiences will respond differently to you. Cultural and religious sensitivities must be considered – more so because you are a woman.

Plan how you are going to dress, how you are going to enter the room and your posture. Practice your speech. Ask a friend to record you rehearsing your full presentation. Then, self-critique your performance. If you are the person giving a critique for a friend, always give positives first to build their confidence.

Break up your presentation into distinct parts – an opening, middle and closing – and practice the talk in those separate parts. In the morning, practice your opening; in the afternoon, practice the points in the middle; at night, practice your closing. When you tackle each section individually, it's much easier to master. When Lori has to deliver a talk, she uses her driving time to go through it section by section. By the end of the day, she's gone through all the sections, and at night she can merge everything together in front of the mirror.

Rehearsals with your slides are important so that you can practice how you're going to talk about each slide, as well as the transition from one slide to the next. Being well rehearsed and well prepared gives you a huge confidence boost when it comes to delivering your talk.

Don't read to your audience. This isn't storybook hour. They didn't come to hear you read your slides to them; they came to hear you talk. A bullet point shouldn't be explaining the idea – it should only represent it. You elaborate. Try to memorize what you need to say. You'll lose your audience very quickly if you're too focused on your slides and not on the people listening. It also gives the message that you're unprepared. If you need to, use notes to glance at, but keep your eyes more on the audience than on your notes.

And no matter how great a speaker you are, and how conversant you are with your subject, you can't wing it. Rather, practice your presentation ahead of time and perfect the message and delivery. It's a reflection of your regard for your audience.

Don't forget to rehearse at the venue, too. Be there early so you can check your equipment and rehearse. You need to know that your voice carries to all areas of the room or that the sound and projection equipment is working as it should. Carry an extra set of speakers if you have to and bring every possible adaptor you might need. It's also a really good idea to have your own remote slide changer because they're all different and using one you're familiar with is a great stress reducer. When you hold a remote, it also prevents you from fidgeting.

Ask someone to sit in various areas of the room and run through a few sentences to be sure they can hear you. Be aware of any noisy equipment, such as coolers, air conditioners, fans, or activities in a nearby room or hall, that may require you to step up the volume. If you need to handle unexpected noises during your presentation, go to a table discussion or initiate an activity for the group while the noise passes.

If you're using a microphone, make sure you know how to use it. If you have a handheld microphone, be aware that holding it too close can result in a muffled and irritating vocal projection...but it probably needs to be held closer to your mouth than you think. Test it out!

EXERCISE: VOCAL WARM-UPS

The depth and quality of your speaking voice contribute to the effectiveness of your presentation and are important indicators of how confident you are. When you are nervous, your breathing often becomes quick and shallow, making your voice higher. Breathing, humming, articulating and practicing make a noticeable difference in lowering the vocal register and help you come across more authoritatively. Here are some vocal warm-ups to practice before your presentation:

- Repeat these vowel combinations:
- *Hamm amm amm Hemm emm emm Himm imm imm Homm omm omm Humm umm umm*
- Say this phrase fast and as many times as you can: "Unique New York. Unique New York."

One of the most common ways we see people tripping themselves up in presentations is through the excessive use of fillers. Those "ums," "ahs" and "you knows" are the hallmarks of inexperienced or nervous public speakers.

Often people are not aware of the extent to which they use fillers. To become more conscious of how often you use fillers, you can film yourself while giving a presentation, record your voice on your phone or have a friend or a trusted colleague watch you rehearse. Most of us are surprised (sometimes even shocked) by how often we fill our speech with unnecessary words. But, when we know about it, we can fix it. We tend to use fillers when we need to give ourselves a chance to think, when we're searching our minds for the right thing to say, when we don't have a ready response or when we're transitioning from one thought to another. The more prepared we are, the better we know our subject and the more present and focused we are in the room, the less we need to throw out an "um" to fill the blanks.

And remember that a strategically placed pause is one of the most powerful non-verbal tools we have. A pause can add emphasis to an important point. A pause can give your audience the chance to absorb the information you are communicating. And in the event that you forget your words or make a mistake, pretend it's actually a well-rehearsed pause, or come back with a quip such as, "Let me reconnect my mind to my mouth," or, "Let me rephrase that."

A well-placed pause also presents an opportunity to make eye contact with the members of your audience. Making consistent eye contact with the audience reinforces your authority and sincerity and helps create a true connection. If your audience numbers are in the hundreds or thousands, focus on a few individuals in various areas of the room. Although you're gazing in a general area, it gives a much more personal feel, as if you are looking at many people and not just the one person you are focusing on. Some professionals have been told to stare at the back of the room in large presentations, but that conveys a sense that you are looking past the audience and not connecting with them. Eye contact is all about making connection and creating engagement.

As we discussed in Chapter 2, UCLA Professor Albert Mehrabian found that over 90% of the way a message is received is through non-verbal cues, so it's not only our eye contact that we need to be conscious of; it's our body language, too. Pull out that video camera again and watch how you move when you're talking or delivering a presentation. Notice which poses, movements or actions enhance your presence and which ones detract from it.

Use your body and your space to your advantage. Start by standing tall. Take a deep breath and move your ribcage up – it works wonders for your posture.

Be aware of your stance. Standing with your feet together makes you look like a tapered candle that can be tipped over. Instead, stand with your hips parallel to your feet. This is called "being rooted," and gives the impression of a grounded, confident individual. Take up space in the room; physically use different areas of the room and be purposeful with your movements and body language.

When you're speaking, movement is perfectly acceptable as long as you do so with purpose. Don't walk backwards from your audience because it saps energy; rather walk with the purpose of connecting with the audience. Many people have the unconscious habit of rocking from side to side or taking constant steps – don't do it. It will make you look nervous and you'll make everyone else dizzy. If you need to, film yourself in your preparation phase so that you can become aware of your movements and work on planting your feet firmly on the ground.

One very effective move is to take two or three steps before pausing to ground your position. Then take a couple more steps again, pause and ground your position. To keep the rhythm going, think, "Step, step, pause. Step, step, pause."

Taking timed steps is also a way to control the pacing of your presentation. While you don't want to present information so quickly that your audience has trouble following, you also don't want to be too slow, especially when it comes to slideshow presentations. Keeping any one slide up too long is a sure-fire way to lose the attention of your audience. Recording and timing your presentation in advance is a good strategy to ensure that your pacing is just right for the audience.

Crossing your arms is a defensive posture that creates a distance between you and your audience. It can also give your audience the impression that you're apathetic about the information you're delivering. We recommend that you use gesture to reinforce a point – mid-level gestures work best. If you gesticulate above your shoulders, it may be distracting for your audience. Hands above the head are great for workouts and air traffic control, but not for professional presentations. And, while wild hand-waving makes you look like you are a little out of control, tight fists, hand smacks and assertive chopping movements can make you look threatening and aggressive. If you keep your hands below your hips, people won't notice them. Keep them above your hips (but below your head) and use your hands to add vitality to your message.

Open hand movements convey a sense of power. On an unconscious level, they also tell your audience that you come in peace, as you couldn't possibly be harboring a weapon. Palms facing up signal that you are inviting, but humble. If you steeple your hands, you are conveying a combination of power and humility. And if you strike a pose with your palms facing up in front of you, it communicates a sense of openness.

You can also watch for non-verbal cues in your audience to understand and connect with them more effectively. Tracey Webster, who studied drama, tells us how she uses that knowledge to modulate the pitch of her voice and present herself. "These are life skills you take wherever you go – eye contact, listening and really tuning in to how your audience is perceiving you," she says. "One of the key skills is listening and learning how to perceive other people's body language. For example, in a presentation, watch if people fold their arms, look at their watches. If you are losing them, how can you get them back and hook them in? Should I speed up my presentation? Cut out some slides and move into a discussion instead? Listen to your gut. Read your audience and tell the story in a way that will make them listen."

And, unless you are talking about a very somber topic or delivering bad news, don't forget to smile. When you begin your presentation with a smile, your audience will receive your message more willingly. A fixed smile can start to look like a grimace (not a good look), but interaction is key for a remarkable presentation – so do try to keep flashing a genuine smile here and there throughout your presentation. People respond to smiles.

As long as you are confident that you have included all the relevant information and action steps that your presentation requires, don't be concerned if your speech seems too short. Nobody ever complains about short presentations. Start on time and end early. Leave them wanting more, not dying of boredom.

If you don't know something, be prepared to admit your ignorance, but say it with confidence. It shows your humanity, and it opens the door for other people to come through with their ideas and their lessons. When it comes to answering questions from the audience, acknowledge and thank the person for raising a concern and be as short and succinct with your answer as possible. Do your homework about your audience and speak directly to their needs.

Above all things, delivering a powerful, compelling presentation is about being passionate and authentic, because if you are contrived and insincere, it shows. The most important thing is to be yourself.

OWN YOUR SLIDESHOW

Have you ever heard of the phrase *death by PowerPoint*? When you get it wrong, nothing can bomb your presentation more than software glitches. But, when you get it right, you can illustrate your message, animate your idea and have the audience's undivided attention.

How exactly do you get that right? We've collected tips from the best presenters in the world, including the TED stage (www.ted.com), on how to create a powerful presentation. Let's start with some of Akash Karia's most useful tools from his book *How to Design TED-Worthy Presentation Slides*.

HOW TO APPROACH A SLIDESHOW PRESENTATION

Karia says the most common mistake people make when approaching a presentation is dumping their entire speech from a Word document onto their slides. The terribly dull result is a "slideument" (a word invented by presentation guru Garr Reynolds) – an awkward hybrid of a PowerPoint presentation and a text-heavy Word document.

Slides should only be used to enhance your message. The objective of using slides is to create a better experience for your audience, not to help you remember what you have to say. Don't confuse slides with giant cue cards for yourself. When it comes to designing your slides, Karia says you should ask yourself, *Am I including this slide to help my audience or to help myself?*

The first step in the design of your presentation is your key message. What is the one single idea you want your audience to remember? What is the single most important idea they need to take away from your presentation? Use your key message as if it's the DNA of your presentation – use it to help you decide what to keep in and what to exclude.

HOW TO DESIGN YOUR SLIDES

Your slides need to look better than good. They need to look fantastic! Your audience is going to judge you and your talk on the quality of your slides. Everything counts. It's the same principle we discussed in Chapter 2 in relation to your physical presence. Everything about you communicates something about yourself – and, yes, that includes the look of your presentations.

If your slides are obvious and unimaginative, they portray a negative message about you. If you couldn't be bothered with putting in a little time and effort to create something inspiring, how can you expect your audience to be inspired about what you have to say? Professionally designed slides portray the message that you have put in time and effort to craft an appealing presentation, and your audience will be more enthusiastic about listening to you.

Keep to one idea per slide and remember that a picture is worth a thousand words. So, wherever possible, use striking visuals to represent your idea. As Julia Lazarus says, "we consistently need to look for creative and entertaining means of delivery, and avoid using clichéd images – such as a handshake to represent teamwork. Be creative and selective in the images you use. And don't pull low-resolution images off the Web; they're only going to pixilate and make your presentation look substandard."

Don't clutter your slides with text – it looks awful and ends up being incredibly distracting for your audience because they'll stop focusing on you to read the slides. In Karia's book, professional speaker Craig Valentine explains this beautifully, "If you and your slides are saying the same thing, one of you is not needed."

Karia suggests using post-it notes to help you design and structure your presentation. According to the *Harvard Business Review*'s blog, using post-it notes for storyboarding your presentation is particularly useful because "the small space forces you to use simple, clear words and pictures. There's no reason to crowd them. This sketching process will help you clarify what you want to say and how you want to say it." Once you have your notes, you can move them around until you find the perfect flow and structure.

Then there's marketing executive and speaker Guy Kawasaki's 10-20-30 slideshow rule. He says a slideshow presentation should have no more than 10 slides, last no longer than 20 minutes, and have no text that's smaller than a 30-point font. He says it doesn't matter whether your idea will revolutionize the world; you still need to spell out the important nuggets in just a few minutes and a couple of slides – each with no more than several words.

Research tells us that audience attention drops considerably after ten minutes of listening to a presentation. If you want to keep your audience engaged, involve them in your presentation. Give them questions to think about. When Lori gives her talk on the myth of work-life balance, she asks the audience questions throughout the presentation, like "How many of you get enough sleep? How many of you are with me right now, or are you thinking about what you have to get done today?" This enables the audience to refocus and stay involved.

Another great tool to keep your audience engaged is to include videos or sound bites. These elements, especially when they're deeply motivating or humorous, keep the energy levels up. And if you're going to include clips, remember to embed the video and sound files into your slideshow file itself (you don't want to disrupt the flow by stopping to open and close files in the middle of your talk).

HAVE CONFIDENCE TO BE THE BEST VERSION OF YOURSELF

Some people are naturally gifted speakers. You might not see yourself as one, but we can all be better and incrementally more effective than we are right now. This is the case even if you are so nervous about speaking in public that you break into a cold sweat at the thought.

There are many fears that hold us back from speaking—from secretly believing that our contribution is worthless, to the fear that we'll look like fools, or that we don't really deserve to be there. If you have fears or self-confidence issues that keep you from stepping into the spotlight and showing just how capable and valuable you really are, it's time to step right back into Chapter 1 and PEMD. Yes, that again. Why do we keep reminding you about it? Because it's such an incredibly powerful and versatile tool. Recalling and visualizing positive past experiences allows success to vibrate within you and serves as a pretty effective antidote to nerves and fear.

Here's the story of the development of one of our trainees:

Before training with us, Samantha struggled with nerves every time she had to make an executive-level presentation. She was annoyed with herself because she knew that it was stopping her from being able to present herself in the best light. She liked the idea of building a PEMD and spent a lot of time building a vivid and detailed PEMD that she could recall at will.

Samantha told us that her first post-training meeting was entirely different. She exuded the confidence and authenticity that came with the memories of her PEMD. It was as if the confidence just flooded back and she proceeded to deliver the information in absolute comfort and in her zone. She found that she stood with authority, that she felt centered and was able to make calm, direct eye contact. She also took it a step further by developing an intelligent, well-thought-out hook to engage her audience.

She was immediately seen as confident, competent and capable – and it directly resulted in a promotion to a higher level of management. In fact, whenever Samantha sees us, she makes a point of saying that she owes the continuing success of her career to these incremental changes. Another way to combat nerves and boost your confidence before giving a talk is to visualize it. Right before your talk, take a quiet moment and get away from everyone else so that you can focus on your talk and visualize yourself delivering that talk. Visualize yourself opening and closing powerfully, an enraptured audience, and your talk making a difference in someone's life.

Jayshree Naidoo, whose passion is nurturing young entrepreneurs, reminds us, "You are the subject matter expert or the thought leader for that specific moment in time. The audience or attendees will draw their knowledge from you on the day. Only you know if you leave something out in your presentation. Don't try and fix it during your presentation time, rather weave it into the answers you give during the Q&A section."

It's incredibly important to start becoming more mindful of what internal dialogue is going on, what messages you are sending to yourself. Before a presentation, a meeting with a higher-up, or a job interview, check in with yourself and delete the negative self-talk and replace it with thoughts and affirmations such as, *I have a right to be here. I have something valuable to contribute. I deserve to be here.* And then breathe. Deep, rhythmic breathing is a simple and effective way to help you calm down, focus, and access your internal confidence.

Combine all this with a relaxed tone of voice, strong projection and clothes that have structure, and you can create an impression of stature, credibility and confidence. When you're fully prepared and fully mindful, you're in the best position to step into that room and own your podium.

OWN YOUR PODIUM...IN A FLASH

- Meetings and presentations are golden opportunities to show your strengths in a public forum. Take full advantage of them.
- Develop a strong hook that will grab your audience within the first few seconds. It can be a question, a compelling statement or a fascinating fact.
- Make your presentation relevant to your audience. What's in it for them? Ask what you want people thinking, feeling and doing (TFD).

- Share great anecdotes to drive your message home.
- Finish with confidence and certainty. The way you end is as important as the way you begin. Give your audience a call to action.
- Prepare. Prepare. Prepare. Know your audience, research your content. Rehearse your speech. Check your equipment.
- If you're using a slideshow, only use your slides to enhance your message. Don't clutter your slides with text, keep one idea per slide and remember that a good picture can be worth a thousand words.
- Use Guy Kawasaki's 10-20-30 slideshow rule: 10 slides, 20 minutes talking and no text smaller than a 30-point font.
- Use your Positive Emotional Memory Database to build confidence and combat nerves.
- Lose fillers such as "ah," "um" and "you know."
- Use strategically placed pauses for dramatic effect.
- Use your body and your space to your advantage. Stand tall with your hips parallel to your feet.
- Make eye contact. Smile.

10
WORDS FROM WOMEN WHO
OWN IT

Knowledge is power? No. Knowledge on its own is nothing, but the application of useful knowledge, now that is powerful.

– ROB LIANO

Our research included interviews with some remarkable individuals. It was an honor to speak to so many women with unique experiences of business success and who were very willing to share their journeys, their strengths, their philosophies, and their insights. Our interviewees were as fearless about sharing their failures and vulnerabilities as they were about sharing their successes and what helped them get there.

We have been so pleased with the generosity of the women who took part and the quality of their advice that we've put together a compilation of quotes for you in this final chapter. Every quote is a gleaming gem of wisdom.

ON BEING A WOMAN IN BUSINESS

We're so hard on ourselves, and hold ourselves to such a high standard. It's important to remember that emotional health requires you to be kind and gentle to yourself.

Cynthia Good, Founder and Owner, Little PINK Book

Whatever we do, individually or collectively, 50% of the people will like it, and 50% won't. The trick is to get to 51%. You don't have to satisfy everyone – and women try too hard to do that. Men know it's not going to happen, and they navigate through it without worrying about it.

Carolyn Jackson, Senior Vice President, Human Resources, Coca Cola

The majority of women I've worked with are brilliant and capable and could run circles around many, many people, but their greatest flaw is their lack of confidence. The irony is business leaders are just dying for someone to have a confident point of view that might not be echoing what they think.

Linda Brenner, Founder of Talent Growth Advisors

My two main career paths have been in industries which are largely male-dominated. It would be naive to think that people don't look at you as a woman. It is for that reason that I have always worked harder and smarter and with more integrity than all of my colleagues. The most important lesson is to know your business and learn from everyone, even from those who irritate you.

Rogany Ramiah, Human Resources Director at Massdiscounters

Do not look for reasons to be undermined. Don't use being a woman as a reason to be undermined and then play the victim. There is no reason for that. Use your femininity to your advantage, and do not be afraid to have multiple roles in your life. Do not be afraid to say, "I want it all – I want a career and I want a family." I have that role and I am proud of it.

Nikki Cockcroft, online retailing expert

Free yourself. This is the workplace. You have not been appointed because of your gender. You have been appointed because of your brain, your competence and your skills. Give yourself permission to be rewarded for what you bring to the table.

Redi Tlhabi, 702 talk show host and author

ON BEING A LEADER

I make it a point to treat everyone with dignity and respect. Then, even when they're older, they know I appreciate their experience. I tell them I don't want to make any mistake I don't have to make, and I'm trying to live vicariously through them. They know that I value them, and their feedback and input.

Michelle Livingstone, Vice President of Transportation, Home Depot

When you're operating within the context of an organization, no matter what the industry, make sure you understand that industry well, understand what the success factors are, understand the financials and the levers that are pulled within that business. Why? Because if you understand that, then you can figure out how to connect what you're an expert at to those outcomes. And that's when it makes a difference, that's when you have credibility.

Arlette Guthrie, Human Resources Vice President,
non-store, The Home Depot

Being a leader is a privilege. You are there to remove obstacles and make the road ahead as smooth as velvet. Your colleagues need to feel that you are there to enable their success. I believe my colleagues are my clients. I meet deadlines and meet my commitments. Consistency, delivery, sincerity, and love are some of the most important leadership traits.

Grace Harding, Company Leader of the Ocean Basket Group

ON WHAT LEADERS LOOK FOR IN YOU

Number one is integrity. I always tell people never compromise yourself, even on the little things. If I tell you I'm going to do something and I can't, you'll hear back from me about why I couldn't do it.

Becky Blalock, author speaker and
Managing Partner at Advisory Capital

I'm definitely looking for positive thinkers and a can-do attitude, but I recognize that you have to have a diverse team, including diversity of thought and leadership approaches. I also look for analytical and problem-solving skills and proven leadership skills, either in the workforce or in volunteer work.

Michelle Livingstone, Vice President of Transportation, Home Depot

Make yourself available to work with whomever, on whatever. It's not about you; it's about others who see you as a tool to get things done. In the process, they help you and they teach you. Next thing you know, they'll be giving you more projects and more responsibility.

Carolyn Jackson, Senior Vice President, Human Resources, Coca Cola

Bring your personality to work – a lot of people check their personality at the door and bring in this corporate/work persona. Bring all of who you are to work, build meaningful relationships at work, have fun and work hard, and you will walk out of the office saying that was a really great day.

Tracey Webster, former CEO of the African Leadership Institute, CEO of the Branson Centre of Entrepreneurship and co-founder of the Starfish Foundation

I look for people who have innate potential, optimism, and the ability to do things. I look for a sense of energy that you know will be contagious, and I look for people who can be part of a collective, because you're not going to do anything on your own. I also look for people who are positive about continuous learning and who apply it, people who are open to doing something 18 months from now that's completely different from what they're doing now.

Yaarit Silverstone, Senior Partner, Accenture.

I look for an enquiring, curious mind and tenacity. A person with problem- solving skills and a can-do attitude, who must be able to pick him- or herself up and move ahead no matter what the challenge. Solutions-driven. A person who will take responsibility for solving problems and not wait for others to fix it for them.

Gisèle Wertheim Aymés, Owner and Publisher of Elle, Elle Decoration SA and Longevity brands

ON FOLLOWING THE VISION

Create a vision for yourself and then outline the goals and steps you need to take to achieve that vision. Don't be deterred by what other people think or say, and always look for the road less travelled. Always consider what your highest values are when planning your vision.

Joan Joffe, founder of Joffe Associates

I love to dance, but I never allowed myself to explore that, until I recently realized it doesn't matter what people think because I've already achieved a level of success. So now I'm doing a lot of dance, and it's fulfilling. It's a chance to share something that I'm very passionate about.

Cynthia Good, founder and owner, Little PINK Book

The most important advice I can give is to have a vision and be true to what that vision is. Every year, I create a new vision for myself, but I unpack it into little baby steps. I always have a gratitude journal, and what I have learned in that week or month contributes towards my big, audacious goal. I love reflecting over my life, which includes my career and family. It helps me see what I have missed and what my blind spots are. This takes complete discipline. Reflection is extremely important to further your journey as this helps you approach your next step by learning from past experiences.

Koo Govender, Group CEO of VWV

I think everybody has a dream, so whatever your dream is, go for it, and see if you can make it happen. If you are trying for your dream, then you will work with much more passion and enthusiasm.

Jenni Newman, CEO of JNPR

ON WORK-LIFE INTEGRATION

Work-life balance is about the choices you make at home and the choices you make at work. I think the type of person you marry is extremely important. I feel that I am a better person for working, as I show my two daughters that a woman can have both a successful career and be an attentive mother. Balance is about saying no and acknowledging what doesn't bring me joy. The best advice I have received on achieving balance came from my coach. She told me, "If you go into this challenge assuming you have to trade off your work to get personal balance, that's exactly what you'll end up doing. But, if you approach the situation telling yourself, *I can have it all*, then you will have it all." You need to decide what work-life balance looks like for you. It's about being very specific when it comes to the things that make you feel like you've got enough balance in your life.

Andrea Quaye, Marketing Director at SAB

For me there has never been a debate about being a mother *or* a career woman. There was never a debate about one or the other. It has always been about how to be both. The key is to be present wherever you are. So when you are being a wife, be a wife. When you are with your children, be the mother. When you are at work, work – be present, appreciate what is happening around you, and share the moment wherever you are.

Nikki Cockcroft, Group Head of Online at Woolworths

ON SUCCESS, DECISIONS AND FAILURE

On Success: Change is scary, especially for women, who fall into a trap because society has very narrow ideas about what constitutes success. If you're attractive, wealthy and visible you're successful. But that's not how I'd define it. For me, it's about personal happiness.

On Failure: We need to reassess and reinvent many times during our lives. There are those times, like when you graduate from college, or when you get to a certain point in your first job, you reassess, and do a lot of soul searching, which is hard work, but hopefully something resonates and you start again to rebuild.

Cynthia Good, Founder and Owner, Little PINK Book

We all know someone who has been fired, dismissed, laid off or whatever you want to call it. The ones who survive recognize that it's all good. It's all OK. It's painful because it's just always such a surprise, but there's always a lesson there.

Linda Brenner, Managing Partner, Talent Growth Advisors

We have more of an emotional connection to failure than men do. Perhaps it's in our psyche as little girls. We have been taught to grow up without failure, and to be accepted is to be perfect. We aren't encouraged to fail. I wonder if we have big enough visions for our own lives. I wonder how many women say they want to be the president. Why don't we? I feel our dreams are way too small. We need to dream big dreams and never stop working towards realizing them.

Tracey Webster, former CEO of the African Leadership Institute,
CEO of the Branson Centre of Entrepreneurship and
co-founder of the Starfish Foundation

I've had setbacks – with my health and with my career. But setbacks are just setting you up for your comeback. And working through the challenges gives you more credibility and authenticity.

Melissa Dawn Simkins, brand guru and President of Velvet Suite

I do not know anybody who is prominent and successful and has not had a challenge in their lives or dealt with anxiety. And when those people share their stories, they affirm my humanity. They make me cut myself some slack for the times when I don't know what to do.

Redi Tlhabi, 702 talk show host and author

Even if your opinion is wrong, at least it's an opinion. You become amazing when you are willing to be accountable for something.

Anele Mdoda, 94.7 drive host, TV presenter and media personality

Start with the end in mind. You need to be intentional in everything you do. Who has time not to be? Think of the longer term goal and then build the stepst that will take you there. As you conduct your work, think [whether] what you are doing takes you any closer to what you want to accomplish. If not, reconsider.

Beatriz Rodriguez, Director and Chief Diversity Officer, The Home Depot

ON THE BENEFIT OF HINDSIGHT

The lesson I didn't learn until way too late in life was it is not what you produce, it's how well you can collaborate. Period. It doesn't matter if your work is the best there is; you have to be able to work well with people.

Linda Brenner, Founder of Talent Growth Advisors, and
Former Director of Retail Staffing a Home Depot

I was so nervous about taking that next step. You don't know what's going to happen, and you can let fear stop you. But don't be afraid. Things work themselves out.

Nima Ahmed, Director of Programming at CNN

When you're first starting out, you don't see where the silver lining is going to come from. I would have told my younger self that the hard work will pay off.

Johanna Mukoki, CEO of TWF Travel

I used to be in the position where I thought it was impossible to be a senior woman leader. I would tell the younger Koo, *You can do it*. Your failures are just experiences, so continually embrace yourself with self- confidence.

Koo Govender, Group CEO of VWV

Be the best you that you can be in whatever you do, every day. Be true to yourself. This is about being authentic. Be careful of living to please others first; you can forget who you are in the process. If you try to be everything to everyone, you could end up being nothing to anyone.

Rogany Ramiah, Human Resource Director at Massdiscounters

I think I would tell the younger me not to be intimidated, to trust in my instinct and not to try so much to convince people of my capabilities, but to quietly assert myself.

Pheladi Gwangwa, 702 Station Manager

What I would say to my younger self is that all your dreams and ambitions of a big, full, exciting life are yours for the taking. If you can believe it, you can achieve it. Stop asking how it's going to happen or who is going to help you get there. What's important is to focus on the journey and not the goal.

Amy Kleinhans-Curd, current businesswoman and former Miss South Africa

In terms of advice for my younger self, I'd say there are two things I tell folks. One is as I was going up the career ladder I did well because I stayed in my field of study and I have no regrets, but on the other hand, I didn't make some of the cross-functional opportunities I had. I should have taken those risks and been a little more adventurous to help myself round out.

Michelle Livingstone, Vice President of Transportation,
The Home Depot

With hindsight, I could have spent time standing up for myself more. Sometimes I let other people win because challenging them was too much of a fuss. And I've got a very strong personality, so sometimes I feel like I need to keep myself in check so that I don't intimidate people. I don't think that's a bad thing if it's done for the right reasons, and if you're allowing someone's voice to also be heard. But I think I did it because I was afraid that I was earning a reputation as the fussy girl who is always challenging and questioning. But you know what? There's nothing wrong with that.

Redi Tlhabi, 702 talk show host and author

Be kind to yourself and just move on when you make a mistake. Don't take yourself too seriously.

Judy Dlamini, Executive Chair of the Mbekani Group

Have a mentor and be a mentor. I would not be here today if it wasn't for the mentors who trusted me, encouraged me and celebrated with me each of my accomplishments. I owe it to them to do the same for others. And as I mentored others, I've realized that I get more out of that new relationship. It builds my confidence, expands my network, satisfies my curiosity, and makes me feel good about giving back.

Beatriz Rodriguez, Director and Chief Diversity Officer, The Home Depot

ON WOMEN SUPPORTING EACH OTHER
One has to feel confident to ask for help. People don't want to appear stupid, so they resist seeking help. In my work as an Advocacy Skills Trainer, we are trying to teach young lawyers that everybody starts off on a less experienced level. They need to understand that asking for assistance is not a sign of weakness, but rather a sign of proper preparation.

Sharise Weiner, High Court Judge

Women are getting better at supporting each other, but there is still too much cat-fighting instead of a true sisterhood at the office.

Julia Lazarus, strategic consultant for General Electric

It is possible to grow while you lift up others with you. As women, we have to take the time to appreciate the unique challenges we face, and we have to create the right platforms and opportunities to grow other aspiring women who can one day make a difference. Never make another woman feel invisible.

Jayshree Naidoo, head of the Standard Bank Incubator

ON OWNING YOUR SPACE

You've got to be well-researched, you've got to be well-trained, and you have to go the extra mile. Because, to own your space, you can't be average in that space, So, to me, owning it is about the accountability for whatever your space is, whether it is managing the household, ensuring that your kinds have a fantastic education both developmentally and academically, or it's within a corporate environment. And so, if I need additional training, if I need mentors, if I need to ride sidesaddle with someone who's been doing it well before I have, I'm willing to do these things. Effectively owning your space also suggests that you know your shortcomings and know where to enhance or augment what you're bringing to the table.

Arlette Guthrie, The Home Depot

While the inspiration to own your space fully and unquestionably may come from women like those you've read about in this book, the decision to embark on that journey is one only you can make. Inspiration turns into action when you fully commit yourself to the process. We hope our book has given you tools to do just that.

Nadia and Lori

ACKNOWLEDGMENTS

As we all know, without action, determination and support, an idea remains just an idea. So, immense gratitude must go to the many people who assisted us in turning a coffee conversation into *Own Your Space: The Women's Guide to Polish, Poise and Empowerment*.

We would like to start by thanking the very talented Sabine Bittle, our "word stylist", who has successfully articulated our message and interpreted it into its best possible format. You supported our vision from day one and showed relentless passion and commitment to the project. Thank you for the amazing work you have done and for helping us share our message for women to discover their true power. It has been a truly unique experience going on this journey with you as you bring wisdom, professionalism and passion to everything you do.

Thank you to the amazing businesswomen who contributed their time, shared their journeys, and gave us the gifts of their insights. We sincerely hope you all find that this book honors the spirit of your contributions, wisdom and leadership. Our deepest admiration and gratitude goes to:

Gwen Beck, Nikki Cockcroft, Kat Cole, Ambassador Suzan Johnson Cook, Sabine Dall'Omo, Judy Dlamini, Jennifer Dorian, Phumza Dyani, Koo Govender, Pheladi Gwangwa, Grace Harding, Margaret Hirsch, Joan Joffe, Ranka Jovanovic, Amy Kleinhans-Curd, Julia Lazarus, Amy Cuddy, Dr. Colinda Linde, Anele Mdoda, Shamala Moodley, Kokodi Morobe, Johanna Mukoki, Jayshree Naidoo, Dawn Nathan-Jones, Jenni Newman, Naomi Nqweni, Mamokgethi Phakeng, Andrea Quaye, Rogany Ramiah, Emma Sadleir, Melissa Dawn Simkins, Elaine Sterling, Butsi Tladi, Redi Tlhabi, Sylvia Walker, Edith Venter, Tracey Webster, Sharise Weiner, Gisèle Wertheim Aymés, Tara Young and Professor Shirley Zinn.

We would like to thank Pan Macmillan for the opportunity to turn our advice and guidance around truly "Owning It" into a book. Terry Morris, Andrea Nattrass, Babongile Zulu and Laura Hammond, it has been such a fantastic journey with you and we respect your professionalism and integrity. You understood our vision and have given us a platform to reach many more women than we could ever reach in our own training sessions. It has been a true privilege to work with you. To our editor, Kelly Norwood-Young, you are a true master of your craft. Thank you for your guidance and incredible understanding of our vision. It has been an absolute privilege to work with you.

Miriam Lacob Stix, thank you for supporting our project with endless patience and editorial guidance. And to each and every person who has ever attended a Greater Impact Workshop or a Beyond the Dress Event, thank you for being open to continued personal growth and for endorsing the philosophy that all self-development really begins with self-awareness.

As co-authors and collaborators, we each have a long list of individuals to personally thank and acknowledge:

FROM NADIA

My first thank you must go to my partner in this endeavor, Lori Milner. We all know an idea can only become a reality with persistence, tenacity and attention to detail. Lori, thanks for being the Ying to my sometimes chaotic Yang, and for seeing the potential to turn our passion into a product.

Enormous appreciation to my UCT Drama professors, who first introduced me to the concept of Owning Your Space. The ability to truly do so has defined my coaching techniques, and inspired workshop participants and audiences to exude confidence, competence and charisma.

Learning to truly Own Your Space is a journey, and one that is often assisted or thwarted by parents. I won the lottery. Annetta and Morris Bilchik, thank you for encouraging me to address your dinner party guests with performances from my four- to 12-year-old self and for the endless lifts to drama classes and play practices. You were tireless.

And to my dear mother-in-law, Annette Kesler, the doyenne of South African food writers, accomplished author and editor of Showcook.com – thank you not only for your support, but for being a superb example to me and my daughters of truly Owning It, whatever the obstacles.

To each and every headmaster, mentor, coach and teacher who encouraged my theatrics and recognized my potential: Elliot Wolf, Toby Kushlick, Doreen Feitlberg, Della Fuchs, Keith Maker, Liz Mills, Robin Lake, Rudy Nadlir, Nancy Neill, Lynn Wong, Lisa Simms, Nancy Smith, Angelique Vassilatos-Denius, Daphne Schechter, Chuck Reaves, Michelle Livingstone. It takes a village!

To my CNN producers, friends and colleagues who have the confidence to put me on air unscripted. You continue to help me Own It. Josh Levs, Tenisha

Bell, TJ Holmes, Christi Paul, Victor Blackwell, Jason Morell, Nora Zimmett, Michael Heard, Sonja van Sacker, Troy Bentley, I love you guys. To all my clients from Home Depot, Coca-Cola, Turner Entertainment Networks, Institute of Nuclear Power Operations, and CNN, as well as many others. Thank you for each and every opportunity to share my workshops and keynotes with your valuable employees. It is a privilege. To my aunt, dear friend and editor, Miriam Lacob Stix. Thank you for your ability to clarify my thinking and correct my grammar in a long series of newsletters, blogs and my first two books: *The Little Book of Big Networking Ideas* and *Small Changes: Big Impact*. They continue to make a Big Impact on the professional lives of countless participants in my workshops and training sessions.

Finally, Owning Your Daily Space would not be possible or enjoyable without the support of my brilliant business partner and husband, Steve, and my glorious, empowered daughters Alexa and Julia.

I am so happy to share my space with all of you!

FROM LORI

I could not have done this without the love and encouragement of my husband, JJ. Thank you for your unconditional support during this process and for believing in me. I am grateful for your commitment to our family and am proud of the father and husband you are. Thank you for always keeping your sense of humor and giving me the ability to laugh every day. You are my rock and inspire me to become the best version of myself. I love you.

To my beautiful children, Aiden and Noa, you have truly taught me the concept of balance and what the real priorities are in life. You are my light, and you motivate me every day to become the role model you can be proud of.

A special mention has to be made of my brother, Shaun Levitan. Growing up, you taught me the values of self-respect and hard work. You continue to inspire me as a successful entrepreneur, a committed parent and a community leader.

Karen Milner, thank you for absolutely everything you do for me and our family. This journey certainly would not have been possible without your dedication, unconditional love and, of course, the Granny Mobile.

Thank you to my wonderful family and friends for your support and encouragement; your friendship has been instrumental in my journey.

To my special clients, thank you for taking the leap with me and enabling me to inspire and uplift your ladies, and some of your men too.

To Nadia Bilchik, what a ride! You are a true friend and partner. I look forward to our continued journey together. You are an inspiration and an example of someone who owns her space with humility, compassion and confidence.

And, of course, I must go back to where it all began – to my parents, because this is where I got my grounding and values. To my mother, Glenda Levitan, thank you for your tenacity, unconditional love, encouragement, and for always being a pillar of support to me. To my late father, Arnold Levitan, you gave me the greatest gifts to carry with me in my adult life: positivity and the power of choice. Your belief that I could achieve anything has pushed me through the toughest moments of self-doubt and I know how proud you would be of this accomplishment.

REFERENCES AND RECOMMENDED READING

INTERVIEWS

Gwen Beck, Group Employee Benefits Manager Massmart Nikki Cockcroft, Group Head of Online at Woolworths
Kat Cole, CEO of Focus Brands
Sabine Dall'Omo, CEO of Siemens South Africa
Judy Dlamini, Executive Chairman of the Mbekani Group Jennifer Dorian, Senior Manager at Turner Classic Movies
Phumza Dyani, Executive Head of Key Accounts at Vodacom Denise Elsbree Smith, social networking expert
Koo Govender, Group CEO of VWV Pheladi Gwangwa, 702 Station Manager
Grace Harding, Company Leader of the Ocean Basket Group Margaret Hirsch, Chief Operations Officer of Hirsch's
Joan Joffe, founder of Joffe Associates
Troy Allen Johnson, digital strategist at Ambassador Social Media
Suzan Johnson Cook, third Ambassador for International Religious Freedom, US State Department
Ranka Jovanovic, Editorial Director at ITWeb
Amy Kleinhans-Curd, businesswoman and former Miss South Africa Julia Lazarus, strategic consultant for General Electric
Colinda Linde, clinical psychologist; chair Scientific and Advisory Board at SADAG; author Anele Mdoda, 94.7 Drive Host, TV presenter and media personality
Shamala Moodley, head of FNB HR
Kokodi Morobe, former HR Director at Nielsen SA
Johanna Mukoki, CEO of Travel with Flair (TWF) Travel Jayshree Naidoo, head of the Standard Bank Incubator Dawn Nathan-Jones, former CEO of Europcar
Jenni Newman, CEO of JNPR
Naomi Nqweni, Chief Executive of Wealth, Investment Management and Insurance at Barclays Africa Group
Mamokgethi Phakeng, Vice Principal of Research and Innovation at UNISA Andrea Quaye, SAB Marketing Director
Rogany Ramiah, Human Resources Director at Massdiscounters Emma Sadleir, social media law specialist
Melissa Dawn Simkins, US brand guru and President of Velvet Suite Elaine Sterling, Aesthetics School Director of the Elaine Sterling Institute Butsi Tladi, MD of Alexander Forbes Health
Redi Tlhabi, 702 talk show host and author Mario van Tonde, clinical psychologist Edith Venter, owner of Edith Unlimited Sylvia Walker, author and financial planner
Tracey Webster, previously CEO of the African Leadership Institute and CEO of the Branson Centre of Entrepreneurship Sharise Weiner, High Court Judge
Gisèle Wertheim Aymés, owner and Publisher of Elle, Elle Decoration SA and Longevity brands
Tara Young, head of CNN makeup worldwide Shirley Zinn, CEO of Shirley Zinn Consulting

ONLINE RESOURCES

Alessandra, Dr. Tony. "The Platinum Rule (2992)." The Platinum Rule (2992). Accessed February 27, 2017. http://www.alessandra.com/dobusiness.htm.

Batchilder, Rory. "Listening Skills – The 10 Principles of Listening | SkillsYouNeed." October 24, 2013. Accessed February 27, 2017. http://rorybatchilder.com/listening-skills-the-10-principles-of- listening-skillsyouneed/.

Bilchik, Nadia. "The Verbal and Non-Verbal Elements of Speaking for Success." Nadia Bilchik: Speaker, Trainer, Author. September 05, 2008. Accessed February 27, 2017. http://nadiaspeaks.com/2008/09/the-verbal-and-non-verbal-elements-of-speaking-for-success/.

Bilchik, Nadia. "Overcome Nerves and Develop Confidence." Nadia Bilchik. December 17, 2009. Accessed February 27, 2017. http:// nadiaspeaks.com/2009/12/overcome-nerves-and-develop-confidence/.

Brainy Quote. http://www.brainyquote.com/

Brown, Brené "The Power of Vulnerability." TED. June 2010. Accessed February 27, 2017. http://www.ted.com/talks/brene_brown_on_vulnerability.

B-society. http://www.b-society.org/research.

Clark, Dorie and Matthew Turner. "What I Learned from Interviewing 163 Entrepreneurs About Failure." Forbes. 11 February 2015. Accessed February 27, 2017. http://www.forbes.com/sites/dorieclark/2015/02/11/ what-i-learned-from-interviewing-163-entrepreneurs-about-failure/.

Cox, Kelsey. "The Modern Woman's Definition of Success According to LinkedIn." Salon. 11 September 2013. Accessed

February 27, 2017. http://www.salon.com/2013/09/11/the_modern_woman%E2%80%99s_definition_of_success_newscred/

Cuddy, Amy. "Your Body Language Shapes Who You Are." TED. June 2012. Accessed February 27, 2017. http://www.ted.com/talks/amy_cuddy_your_body_language_shapes_who_you_are.

Dilligard, Danica. "Sponsors Crack Glass Ceilings." Financial Times. June 2013, http://www.ft.com/intl/cms/s/0/5135bef4-e4b1-11e2-875b-00144feabdc0.html

Emmons,Robert. "Why Gratitude is Good." The Greater Good: The Science of a Meaningful Life. November 16, 2010. Accessed February 27, 2017. http://greatergood.berkeley.edu/article/item/why_gratitude_is_good.

Falconer, Joel Falconer. "How to Use Parkinson's Law to Your Advantage." Accessed February 27, 2017. http://www.lifehack.org/articles/featured/how-to-use-parkinsons-law-to-your-advantage.html.

Frankel, Dr. Lois. "Get and Keep the Job You Want." Dr. Lois Frankel. October 2003. Accessed February 27, 2017. http://www.drloisfrankel.com/resources/career_transition/june2006getandkeepjobyouwant.pdf.

Peri, Camille. "10 Things to Hate about Sleep Loss." The South African Depression and Anxiety Group. Accessed February 27, 2017. http://www.sadag.org/index.php?option=com_content&view=article&id=2258:10-things-to-hate-about-sleep-loss&catid=39&Itemid=187.

Gonzalez, Maria. "Mindfulness for People Who Are Too Busy to Meditate." Harvard Business Review. March 31, 2014. Accessed February 27, 2017. https://hbr.org/2014/03/mindfulness-for-people-who-are-too-busy-to-meditate/.

Gurian, PhD, Anita. "Gifted Girls – Many Gifted Girls, Few Eminent Women: Why?." Child Study Center. December 13, 2004. Accessed February 27, 2017. http://www.aboutourkids.org/articles/gifted_girls_many_gifted_girls_few_eminent_women_why.

Gurian, PhD, Anita. "Girls with Low Self-Esteem: How to Raise Girls with Healthy Self-Esteem." Child Study Center. April 24, 2014. http://www.education.com/reference/article/Ref_Mirror_Mirror_Wall/?page=2.

Heathfield, Susan M. "Delegation as a Leadership Style: The Art of Successful Delegation." The Balance. April 29, 2016. Accessed February 27, 2017. https://www.thebalance.com/delegation-as-a-leadership-style-1916731.

Hibbert, Christina. "10 Benefits of Practicing Gratitude." Dr. Christina Hibbert. November 17, 2012 Accessed February 27, 2017. http://www.drchristinahibbert.com/10-benefits-of-practicing-gratitude/.

Hughes, Jenni Trent. "Jenni's Top Tips." Sanctuary Spa. 2016. Accessed February 27, 2017. http://www.sanctuary.com/jennitips/.

Hunt-Davis, Ben. "Will It Make the Boat Go Faster?" Speech. 2015. Accessed February 27, 2017. http://www.willitmaketheboatgofaster.com/what-we-do/the-speech/#speech.

Iltman, Ian. "How to Stand Out in a Job Interview and Business Meeting." Forbes. May 26, 2015. Accessed February 27, 2017. http://www.forbes.com/sites/ianaltman/2015/05/26/how-to-stand-out-in-a-job-interview-and-any-business-meeting/2/.

Jacobs, Emma. "Sponsors Crack Glass Ceilings." Financial Times. July 8, 2013. Accessed February 27, 2017. http://www.ft.com/intl/cms/s/0/5135bef4-e4b1-11e2-875b-00144feabdc0.html#axzz3tA8gqkNU.

James, Franke. "Linda Kaplan Thaler on the Power of Nice." Office Politics. February 2006. Accessed February 27, 2017. http://www.officepolitics.com/advice/?p=85.

Janov, Arthur. "Chapter 13: The ABCs of RET (Rational-Emotional Therapy): Holding Back Feelings with Words." Grand Delusions. June 2005. Accessed February 27, 2017. http://www.primaltherapy.com/GrandDelusions/GD13.htm.

Kanter, Rosabeth Moss. "The Imperfect Balance Between Work and Life." Harvard Business Review. August 28, 2012. Accessed February 27, 2017. https://hbr.org/2012/08/the-imperfect-balance-between.html.

King, Donnell. "Four Principles of Interpersonal Communication." 2000. Accessed February 27, 2017. http://www.pstcc.edu/facstaff/dking/interpr.htm.

Kingston, Anne. "Richer, Happier, Fitter? Not for Female Executives." MacLean's. November 12, 2012. Accessed February 27, 2017. http://www.macleans.ca/society/health/the-wealth-health-paradox/.

Knight, MD, Leslie A. "The Power of Asking." Practice Link. Winter 2010, Accessed February 27, 2017. https://journal.practicelink.com/remarks/the-power-of-asking/.

Langer, Ellen Langer. "Mindfulness in the Age of Complexity." Harvard Business Review. March 2014. Accessed February 27, 2017. https://hbr.org/2014/03/mindfulness-in-the-age-of-complexity.

LinkedIn Corporation. "Profile Completeness." LinkedIn. 2017, Accessed February 27, 2017. https://www.linkedin.com/static?key=pop%2Fpop_more_profile_completeness.

Meyerson, Mitch. "5 Steps to Harnessing the Power of Twitter." Entrepreneur. May 19 2015, Accessed February 27, 2017. http://www.entrepreneur.com/article/244213.

Morin, Amy. "5 Ways Resilient People Use Failure to Their Advantage." Forbes. December 14, 2014. Accessed February 27, 2017. https://www.forbes.com/sites/amymorin/2014/12/14/5-ways-resilient-people-use-failure-to-their-advantage/#4dc4cb0b10f8.

The Muse. "6 Tips for Delegating Success." Forbes 23 December 2011. Accessed February 27, 2017. http://www.forbes. com/sites/dailymuse/2011/12/23/6-tips-for-delegating-success/.

National Sleep Foundation. "Study: Physical Activity Impacts Overall Quality of Sleep." National Sleep Foundation. 2017. Accessed February 27, 2017. https://sleepfoundation.org/sleep-news/study-physical-activity-impacts-overall-quality-sleep.

Patel, Sujan. "8 Successful Products That Only Exist Because of Failure." January 16, 2015. Accessed February 27, 2017. http://www.forbes.com/sites/sujanpatel/2015/01/16/8-successful-products-that-only-exist-because-of-failure/.

Peters, Tom. "The Brand Called You." Fast Company. August 31, 1997. Accessed February 27, 2017. http://www. fastcompany.com/28905/brand- called-you.

Porter, Jane. "Yes You Need a Mentor but a Sponsor Will Really Boost Your Career." Fast Company. September 23, 2014. Accessed February 27, 2017. http://www.fastcompany.com/3036037/hit-the-ground-running/ yes-you-need-a-mentor-but-a-sponsor-will-really-boost-your-career.

Restauri, Denise. "5 Qualities of Charismatic People: How Many Do You Have?" Forbes May 3, 2012. Accessed February 27, 2017. https://www.forbes.com/sites/deniserestauri/2012/05/03/5-qualities-of-charismatic-people-how-many-do-you-have/#629ee4172ea9.

Ross, Will. "What is Irrational?" REBT Network. 2006 Accessed February 27, 2017, http://www.rebtnetwork.org/library/ideas.html

Schawbel, Dan. "Sylvia Ann Hewlett: Find a Sponsor Instead of a Mentor." 10 September 2013. Accessed February 27, 2017, http://www.forbes.com/sites/danschawbel/2013/09/10/sylvia-ann-hewlett-find- a-sponsor-instead-of-a-mentor/.

Schilling, Dianne. "10 Steps to Effective Listening." Forbes. November 9, 2012. February 27, 2017. http://www.forbes. com/sites/womensmedia/2012/11/09/10-steps-to-effective-listening/.

Simmons, Rachel. "The Curse of the Good Girl: Raising Authentic Girls with Courage and Confidence." Rachel Simmons. 2017. Accessed February 27, 2017. http://www.rachelsimmons.com/books-and-tv/curse-of-the-good-girl/.

Smith, Craig. "By the Numbers: 125+ Amazing LinkedIn Statistics." Expanded Ramblings. July 30, 2015. http:// expandedramblings.com/index.php/by-the-numbers-a-few-important-linkedin-stats/.

Taylor, Lynn. "How to Be Assertive, Not Aggressive." Psychology Today. May 4, 2013. Accessed February 27, 2017. https://www.psychologytoday.com/blog/tame-your-terrible-office-tyrant/201305/how-be-assertive-not-aggressive.

Warner, Judith. "Fact Sheet: The Women's Leadership Gap." Center for American Progress. March 7, 2014. Accessed February 27, 2017. https://www.americanprogress.org/issues/women/reports/2014/03/07/85457/fact-sheet-the-womens-leadership-gap/.

Waymon, Lynne. "Networking Mistakes that Hurt Your Business: An Interview with Lynne Waymon." http://www. raintoday.com/library/podcasts/networking-mistakes-that-hurt-your-business-an-interview-with-lynne-waymon/.

WPB Expert. "Sponsors vs. Mentors: What's the Difference?" Women Powering Business. February 24, 2014. Accessed February 27, 2017. http://blogs.randstadusa.com/womenpoweringbusiness/sponsors-vs-mentors-whats-the-difference/.

Young, Scott H. "18 Tips for Killer Presentations." Lifehack. 2015. Accessed February 27, 2017. http://www.lifehack.org/articles/communication/18-tips-for-killer-presentations.html.

Zen Quotes. http://zenquotes.org/.

Zwilling, Martin. "How to Delegate More Effectively in Your Business." Forbes. October 2, 2013. Accessed February 27, 2017. https://www.forbes.com/sites/martinzwilling/2013/10/02/how-to-delegate-more-effectively-in-your-business/#27a51f7b69bc.

PUBLICATIONS

Alessandra, Dr. Anthony J. *Charisma: Seven Keys to Developing the Magnetism That Leads to Success.* New York: Warner Books, 2000.

Amoruso, Sophia. *#GirlBoss.* New York: Penguin Books, 2014.

Barsh, Joanna and Susie Cranston *How Remarkable Women Lead: The Breakthrough Model for Work and Life.* New York: Crown Business. 2009.

Barsh, Joanna and Johanne Lavoie. *Centered Leadership.* New York: Crown Business 2014.

Bilchik, Nadia. *The Little Book of Big Networking Ideas: A Guide to Expert Networking.* Atlanta: Greater Impact Publishing, 2013.

Bilchik, Nadia and Kat Cole (2013) *Small Changes: Big Impact.* Atlanta: Greater Impact Publishing, 2013.

Brown, Brené. *I Thought It Was Just Me (But It Isn't).* New York: Gotham Books, 2007.

Brown, Brené. *Daring Greatly: How the Courage to Be Vulnerable Transforms the Way We Live, Love, Parent and Lead.* New York: Penguin Books, 2013.

Cabane, Olivia Fox. *The Charisma Myth: How Anyone Can Master the Art and Science of Personal Magnetism*. New York: Penguin Books, 2013.

Canfield, Jack L. Mark Victor Hansen, Maida Rogerson, Martin Rutte, and Tim Clauss. *Chicken Soup for the Soul at Work*. Deerfield Beach, FL: Health Communications, Inc., 2001.

Canfield, Jack and Janet Switzer. *The Success Principles*. New York: William Morrow, 2009.

Carnegie, Dale *How to Win Friends and Influence People*. New York: Simon and Schuster, 1990.

Cialdini, Robert B. *Influence: Science and Practice*. Upper Saddle River, NJ: Prentice Hall, 2008.

Coleman, Harvey J. *Empowering Yourself: The Organizational Game Revealed*. Bloomington, IN: AuthorHouse, 2010.

Covey, Stephen *The Seven Habits of Highly Effective People*. New York: Free Press, 2004.

D'Allessandro, David. *Career Warfare: 10 Rules for Building Your Successful Brand on the Business Battlefield*. New York: McGraw-Hill, 2008.

Evans, Gail. *Play Like a Man, Win Like a Woman*. New York: Broadway Books, 2000.

Ferrazzi, Keith Ferrazzi and Tahl Raz. *Never Eat Alone: And Other Secrets to Success, One Relationship at a Time*. New York: Doubleday Publishing, 2005.

Ferriss, Timothy. *The 4-Hour Workweek*. New York: Random House, 2007.

Frishman, Rick, Jill Lublin, and Mark Steisel. *Networking Magic: Find the Best – from Doctors, Lawyers, and Accountants, to Homes, Schools and Jobs*. Avon, MA: Adams Media Corporation, 2004.

Futch, Ken. *Take Your Best Shot: Turning Situations into Opportunities*. Atlanta: Wagrub Press, 2005.

Gallo, Carmine. *Talk Like TED*. New York: St Martin's Press, 2014.

Gladwell, Malcolm. *The Tipping Point: How Little Things Can Make a Big Difference*. New York: Back Bay Books, 2002.

Goldsmith, Marshall. *What Got You Here Won't Get You There: How Successful People Become Even More Successful*. New York: Hyperion, 2007.

Goleman, Daniel. *Working with Emotional Intelligence*. New York: Bantam Books, 2002.

Goleman, Daniel *Emotional Intelligence*. New York: Bantam Books, 2005.

Goulson, Mark. *Get Out of Your Own Way: Overcoming Self-Defeating Behavior*. New York: Perigee Trade, 1996.

Goulson, Mark. (2009) *Just Listen: Discover the Secret to Getting Through to Absolutely Anyone*. New York: AMACOM, 2009.

Hewlett, Sylvia Ann. *Executive Presence: The Missing Link Between Merit and Success*. New York: HarperCollins Publishers, 2014.

Hill, Napoleon. *Think and Grow Rich*. Start Publishing LLC, 2013.

Huffington, Arianna. *Thrive*. London: WH Allen Publishing, 2014.

Jennings, Jason Jennings. *Think Big, Act Small: How America's Best Companies Keep the Start-up Spirit Alive*. New York: Penguin, 2012.

Karia, Akash. *How to Design TED-Worthy Presentation Slides*. Akash Karia, 2013.

Akash Karia. *How to Open & Close a TED Talk*. Akash Karia, 2013.

Kay, Katty and Claire Shipman. *The Confidence Code*. New York: HarperCollins Publishers, 2014.

Kehoe, John. *Mind Power into the 21st Century: Techniques for Success and Happiness*. Vancouver, Canada: Zoetic Books, 1997

Kenrick, Douglas T., Noah J. Goldstein, and Sanford L. Braver (eds). *Six Degrees of Social Influence: Science, Application and the Psychology of Robert Cialdini*. New York: Oxford University Press, 2012.

Kida, Thomas E. *Don't Believe Everything You Think: The Six Basic Mistakes We Make in Thinking*. Amherst, NY: Prometheus Books, 2006.

Klaus, Peggy. *Brag! The Art of Tooting Your Own Horn without Blowing It*. New York: Warner Business Books, 2004.

Littell, Robert S. and Donna Fisher. *Power Netweaving: 10 Secrets to Successful Relationship Marketing*. Erlanger, KY: National Underwriting Company, 2001.

Loprinzi, Paul D. and Bradley J. Cardinal. "Association between Objectively- Measured Physical Activity and Sleep, NHANES 2005–2006." *Mental Health and Physical Activity* 4, no. 2 (December 2011): Pages 65–69.

Mackay, Harvey B. *Dig Your Well Before You're Thirsty: The Only Networking Book You'll Ever Need*. New York: Doubleday Publishing, 1999.

Mackay, Harvey B. *Swim with the Sharks Without Being Eaten Alive*. New York: HarperCollins Publishers, 2005.

MacNicol, Glynnis and Rachel Sklar. *The 10 Habits of Highly Successful Women*. Seattle: Lake Union Publishing, 2014.

Marcus, Bonnie *The Politics of Promotion: How High-Achieving Women Get Ahead and Stay Ahead*. Hoboken, NJ: John Wiley & Sons, Inc., 2015.

Marston, William. *Emotions of Normal People*, 5 of 10. London: Taylor & Francis Ltd., 1999.

Mehrabian, Albert. *Nonverbal Communication*. Piscataway, NJ: Transaction Publishers, 2007.

Patterson, Kerry, Joseph Grenny, Ron McMillan, and Al Switzler. *Crucial Conversations: Tools for Talking When Stakes are High*, New York: McGraw Hill, 2011.

Pease, Barbara. *The Definitive Book of Body Language*. New York: Random House, 2006.

Peters, Tom *The Brand You*. New York: Alfred A Knopf, Inc., 1999.

Roane, Susan. *How to Work a Room: The Ultimate Guide to Savvy Socializing in Person and Online*. New York: HarperCollins Publishers, 2000.

Robbins, Tony Robbins. *Awaken the Giant Within: How to Take Immediate Control of Your Mental, Emotional, Physical and Financial Destiny*. New York: Simon and Schuster, 1992.

Robbins, Tony. *Inner Strength: Harnessing the Power of Your Six Primal Needs*. New York: Free Press, 2006.

Ruiz, Don Miguel. *The Four Agreements*. San Francisco: Amber-Allen Publishing, 1997.

Sandberg, Sheryl. *Lean In*. London: WH Allen Publishing, 2013.

Schaefer, Mark. *The Tao of Twitter*. np: CreateSpace, 2011.

Sharp, Timothy. *The Happiness Handbook*. Warriewood, NSW: Finch Publishing, 2008.

Sinek, Simon. *Start with Why*. New York: Portfolio Penguin, 2011.

Stengel, Richard. *Mandela's Way: Lessons on Life, Love and Courage*. New York: Crown Publishing Group, 2010.

Turner, Matthew. *The Successful Mistake: How 163 of the World's Greatest Entrepreneurs Transform Failure and Adversity into Success*. np: Publishizer, 2015.

Wilson, Jerry S. *Managing Brand You: Seven Steps to Creating Your Most Successful Self*. New York: AMACOM, 2008.

Yager, PhD, Jan. *Work Less, Do More: The 14-Day Productivity Makeover*. Stamford, CT: Hannacroix Creek Books, Inc., 2012.

Ziglar, Zig. *See You at the Top*. Gretna, LA: Pelican Publishing Company, Inc., 2000.

TO BOOK NADIA

Nadia is available to speak through

Greater Impact Communication

TRAINING TOPICS INCLUDE:

Maximizing Your Presentation Impact

Presentation skill training to ensure participants are H.E.A.R.D. and that they maximize every presentation opportunity.

Professional/Executive/Leadership Presence

Participants learn tips and techniques, and develop a mindset to project the best version of themselves and understand that everything they do and say communicates.

Brand YOU: Maximize Your Presence & Leverage the Power of Your Personal Brand

Participants learn, develop, communicate, and leverage their unique strengths in a way that benefits both the individual and the business.

What's Your Style?

Learn how your personality impacts your communication.

Bridging Communication Gaps

Learn how to communicate with clarity and confidence in a high-stakes business environment.

Networking for Success

Participants develop techniques and the mindset needed to build value-based and inclusive relationships in a diverse business environment.

Nadia's Keynote Topics Include:

- Unleashing the Power of Your Personal Presence
- Lighting the FIRE: Build Rapport EVERY Time You Communicate
- Kick Your Relationships up a Notch
- Brand You
- Own Your Space: The Woman's Guide to Polish, Poise, and Empowerment

For more information on these and other programs contact:
www.nadiabilchik.com | steve@nadiabilchik.com
404-274-4367

CPSIA information can be obtained
at www.ICGtesting.com
Printed in the USA
BVHW03s0727250318
511516BV00002B/318/P